NEW EDI

A GERMAN VOCAB

The 4500 most useful words
arranged in connected groups suitable
for translation, conversation and composition

E. ERNEST LENTZ
Formerly Modern Language Master
Robert Gordon's College, Aberdeen

BLACKIE London & Glasgow

BLACKIE & SON LIMITED
FURNIVAL HOUSE · 14-18 HIGH HOLBORN ·
LONDON WC1V 6BX

BISHOPBRIGGS · GLASGOW G64 2NZ

BLACKIE VOCABULARIES

By Malcolm W. Murray and E. Ernest Lentz

A FRENCH VOCABULARY
the 3000 most useful words.

By E. Ernest Lentz

A GERMAN VOCABULARY
the 4500 most useful words.

A SPANISH VOCABULARY
the 3500 most useful words.

By M. Kean, M.A.

MEMORANDA LATINA
Word List, Syntax, Idioms and Phrases.

PRINTED IN GREAT BRITAIN BY
THOMSON LITHO, EAST KILBRIDE, SCOTLAND

PREFACE

This is a completely revised edition of the already well-known *German Vocabulary*. In response to great demand it has been completely reset in a modern type instead of its former Gothic script. This change alone will be welcomed by many.

However, since the book was first published many words have gone out of the language and a tremendous number have come into the language—television, record-player, tape-recorder, ballpoint pen, refrigerator, computer, skyscraper, slot-machine, to mention only a few. This has necessitated considerable revision to the content of the vocabulary.

Rather than spoil the arrangement of the book which has proved so successful, Part I contains all of the old edition (brought up-to-date where necessary) and Part II has been added to cope with the major additions. Part II is divided into the same main sections as Part I and numbers are provided which cross-refer with the groups in Part I. Where there was no similar group in the old edition, there is of course no cross-reference.

The major additions come in the field of *The Arts* which now covers theatre, films, radio, television, photography, and all the various sports which were covered only very sketchily in the old edition. Motoring and aviation are also included in this section although they could equally well have been included in the section on travel. We now have more traffic on the roads, therefore some knowledge of traffic signs is necessary and these are given under *Society*. Space travel has become a feature of this age so some words on it are included in *The Universe*.

It is left to the individual how best to work through the vocabulary. You may start at group 1 and work right through to group 418, regardless of the book's division into Parts I and II. You may use only Part I and look to the back, i.e. Part II, for any additions to the various groups. You may wish to look up only words on a certain subject, e.g. telephone, in which case you would look up the Contents which would refer you to the appropriate group or groups in either part.

For people who are not familiar with the old edition, the following advantages of this vocabulary are:

1. Genitive and Plural supplied for every noun in Part I. In new Part II, however, the Genitive is no longer given, except for those masc. and neut. nouns which are stressed on the last syllable and take **-en** all through the declension; the Plural is indicated in all cases except for nearly all fem. nouns which take **-en**, and the great majority of masc. and neut. nouns in **-el**, **-en**, **-er** which do not change.
2. Vowel changes in Irregular Verbs always indicated.
3. All Separable Verbs shown as such.
4. All Intransitive Verbs requiring the auxiliary

sein are marked †. The sign ‡ denotes that a verb sometimes takes *haben* instead of *sein*.

5. For verbs like *danken*, *gedenken*, *anklagen*, all requiring different cases for their objects, and *bitten um*, taking a different preposition in German from English, the necessary information has been supplied.
6. The appendix of dates, numbers, prepositions, adverbial phrases, etc. should be found useful for reference.

E. ERNEST LENTZ

CONTENTS

PART I—groups 1–336; PART II—groups 337–418

EXPLANATION OF CONTRACTIONS

The following examples show how the contractions and signs accompanying the words are to be interpreted:

das Haus, es, ¨er	house (Genitive is **Hauses**, plural is **Häuser**.)
die Mutter, -, ¨-	mother (Genitive is **Mutter**, plural is **Mütter**.)
der Lärm, (e)s, *n.p.*	noise (Genitive is **Lärmes** or **Lärms**, has no plural.)
der Lehrer, s, - (-in)	teacher (Lady teacher = **die Lehrerin**.)
das (Trink)Wasser, s, -	(drinking) water (**Das Wasser** = water, **das Trinkwasser** = drinking water.)
auf-machen	to open (Verb is separable, e.g. **ich mache auf**.)

begegnen† (*dat.*)	to meet (Takes auxiliary **sein** and requires its object in the dative.)
reisen‡	to travel (Usually takes **sein**, but occasionally also **haben.**)
(ein-†)schlafen, ie, a, ä	to sleep (fall asleep) (**Einschlafen** is separable and takes **sein. Schlafen** takes **haben.** Conjugation irregular: imperfect—**schlief ein;** past part.—**eingeschlafen** pres. indic.—**du schläfst ein.**)

In some cases this vowel change is an indication only, there being further irregularities of spelling in the various parts of the verbs, e.g.

sitzen. a, e : **saß, gesessen**
bringen, a, a : **brachte, gebracht**

The only way to know these is to memorize them.

NOTES

1. Feminine nouns in **-in** double the **n** before adding **-en** for the plural.
2. Masculine and neuter nouns in **-nis** double the **s** before adding **-e** for the plural.
3. Nouns in **-ß** form their plural in **-ße** when the vowel is long (**Spāß, ¨ße, Grūß, ¨ße**), and in **-sse** when the vowel is short (**Făß, ¨sser, Flŭß, ¨sse**).

4. In the middle of words **ß** never follows a short vowel, only a long vowel, e.g. **ĕsse, īßt, āßen, gegĕssen.** An apparent exception to this is in compound words. In **flŭßabwärts,** for example, it looks as if the **ß** is in the middle of a word following a short vowel. However there are really two words here (**Fluß** and **abwärts**) and the **ß** is therefore regarded as final. When in doubt medially write **ss**, but never finally.
5. Neuter nouns in **-um** form their plural by changing **um** to **en**, and their genitive singular by adding **-s.**
6. There are no hyphens in German compound words.

PART I

DER MENSCHLICHE KÖRPER—THE HUMAN BODY

1

der Kopf, (e)s, ¨e	head
das Haupt, (e)s, ¨er	head; *also* chief
das Haar, (e)s, e	hair
dunkel	dark
blond	fair
das Gesicht, (e)s, er	face; *also* (eye)sight
schön	beautiful
hübsch	pretty
(lieb)reizend	lovely, (charming)
häßlich	ugly

2

die Stirn, -, en	forehead, brow
das Auge, s, n	eye
blind	blind
die (Sonnen)Brille, -, n	spectacles (sunglasses)
sehen, a, e, ie	to see
an-sehen	to look at (on, upon)
aus-sehen	to look (*have a certain appearance*)
das Aussehen, s, *n.p.*	appearance, mien, look
(un)sichtbar	(in)visible
der Blick, (e)s, e	look, glance

3

der Anblick, (e)s, ***n.p.***	aspect, look
erblicken	to perceive
betrachten	to look at, consider
die Betrachtung, -, en	contemplation
beobachten	to observe
bemerken	to perceive, remark
merkwürdig	remarkable
die Bemerkung, -, en	remark
die Nase, -, n	nose
der Geruch, (e)s, ¨e	smell, odour

4

riechen, o, o (nach)	to smell (of)
wohlriechend	sweet-scented, fragrant
die Wange, -, n	cheek
das Ohr, (e)s, en	ear
hören	to hear
zu-hören (*dat.*)	to listen to
an-hören (*acc.*)	to listen to
horchen (auf ***a.*****)**	to listen (to)
taub	deaf
stumm	mute, dumb

5

das Geräusch, (e)s, e	noise
der Lärm, (e)s, ***n.p.***	noise
die Stille, -, ***n.p.***	silence
schweigen, ie, ie	to be silent
schweigsam	silent
still	silent, quiet
(un)ruhig sein	to keep still (be restless, noisy)
ruhen	to rest
die Ruhe, -, ***n.p.***	rest, quiet
der Mund, (e)s, ¨er	mouth

6

die Lippe, -, n	lip
der Zahn, (e)s, ¨e	tooth
beißen, i, i	to bite
die Zunge, -, n	tongue
sagen	to say, tell
(un)deutlich	(in)distinct
sprechen, a, o, i	to speak
reden (mit)	to talk, speak (to)
an-reden	to address
die Rede, -, n	speech, discourse

7

die Stimme, -, n	voice
laut	(a)loud, loudly
leise	in a low voice, softly
(er)heben, o, o	to raise
schreien, ie, ie	to cry (out)
das Geschrei, (e)s, *n.p.*	cries, screams
der Schrei, (e)s, e	cry
(be)rufen, ie, u	to call (summon)
der Ruf, (e)s, e	shout, call; *also* reputation
aus-sprechen, a, o, i	to pronounce

8

die (Aus)Sprache, -, n	language(pronunciation)
der Geschmack, (e)s, ¨e	taste; *also* flavour
schmecken (nach)	to taste, savour (of)
das schmeckt mir	I like this
kosten	to taste; *also* cost
köstlich	delicious
das Kinn, (e)s, e	chin
der Bart, (e)s, ¨e	beard
die Kehle, -, n	throat
der Hals, es, ¨e	neck

9

die Schulter, -, n	shoulder
der Rücken, s, -	back
die Lunge, -, n	lung
die Brust, -, ¨e	chest, breast
atmen	to breathe
der Atem, s, *n.p.*	breath
der Muskel, s, n	muscle
das Herz, ens, en	heart
herzlich	hearty, heartfelt
der Magen, s, -	stomach

10

die Höhe, -, n	height, stature
hoch	high
groß	great, big, tall
klein	small, little
niedrig	low
stark	strong
schwach	weak
dick	stout; *also* thick
dünn	thin
das (Mit)Glied, (e)s, er	limb (member)

11

der Arm, (e)s, e	arm
die Faust, -, ¨e	fist
der Ell(en)bogen, s, -	elbow
die rechte Hand, -, ¨e	the right hand
die linke Seite, -, n	the left side
(an-)nehmen, a, o, i	to take (receive, accept)
tragen, u, a, ä	to carry; *also* wear
tragbar	portable
der Finger, s, -	finger
der Daumen, s, -	thumb

12

fühlen	to feel, perceive
das Gefühl,[1] (e)s, e	touch, feeling [contact)
(be)rühren[2]	to stir, beat [*eggs*] (touch,
der Sinn, (e)s, e	sense; *also* mind, meaning
der Nagel, s, ¨-	nail
das Bein, (e)s, e	leg
lahm	lame
(ver)lassen, ie, a, ä	to leave, let (abandon)
sich verlassen (auf *a.*)	to rely upon
gehen,† i, a	to go, walk

13

fort-gehen,† i, a	to go away
holen	to go for, fetch
wiederholen	to repeat
holen lassen, ie, a, ä	to send for
kommen,† a, o	to come
bekommen, a, o	to get, receive
der Spaziergang, (e)s, ¨e	walk [walk)
(spazieren) gehen†	to go for a walk (take a
eilen‡	to hasten
sich beeilen	to hasten

14

laufen,‡ ie, au, äu	to run [still, stop)
(stehen) bleiben,† ie, ie	to remain, stay (stand
stehen, a, a	to stand
(sich) halten, ie, a, ä	to hold (oneself)
behalten, ie, a, ä	to keep
die Haltung, -, en	attitude
das Knie, (e)s, e	knee
der Fuß, es, ¨e	foot
die Ferse, -, n	heel
die Zehe, -, n	toe

[1] See also group 161. [2] Cf. Rühreier in group 350.

15

das Fleisch, (e)s, *n.p.*	flesh; meat
fett	fat
mager	lean
die Haut, -, ¨e	skin
scheinen, ie, ie	to look, seem
erscheinen,† ie, ie	to appear
verschwinden,† a, u	to disappear, vanish
der Knochen, s, -	bone
der Nerv, s, en	nerve
nervös	nervous

16

die Ader, -, n	vein
das Blut, (e)s, *n.p.*	blood
sich befinden, a, u	to be (*how or where*)
finden, a, u	to find
die Gesundheit, -, *n.p.*	health
gesund	sound, healthy
wohl	well, in good health
unwohl	unwell, indisposed
gut	good
schlecht	bad

17

übel	evil, wrong, bad
die Krankheit, -, en	illness, disease
krank werden, u, o, i	to become ill, sick
erkranken	to fall *or* be taken ill
die Krankenschwester, -, n	nurse
das Krankenhaus, es, ¨er	hospital
pflegen	to nurse, look after
sorgen (für)	to take care of
die Sorge, -, n	care, attention
die Besorgnis, -, se	care, anxiety

18

sorglos	without care *or* anxiety
vorsichtig	careful, cautious
klug	prudent, clever
der Arzt, es, ¨e (-¨in)	physician, doctor (lady doctor)
der Zahnarzt, es, ¨e	dentist
das Medikament, (e)s, e	medicine
der Apotheker, s, -	chemist, druggist
die Apotheke, -, n	chemist's shop, pharmacy
die Heilung, -, en	cure, healing
heilen	to cure

19

(un)heilbar	(in)curable
genesen,† a, e	to get well (again)
der Schmerz, es, en	pain, grief
schmerzhaft	painful, sore
schmerzlich	painful; grievous
schmerzlos	painless
leiden, i, i (an *d.*)	to suffer (from)
leidend	suffering, ailing
es tut mir leid (um Sie)	I am sorry (for you)
die Kopfschmerzen, *pl.*	headache

20

die Zahnschmerzen	toothache
blaß	pale
bleich	pale, wan
die Ohnmacht, -, en	fainting fit, swoon
zufällig	accidental, casual
(nieder-)fallen,† ie, a, ä	to fall (down)
der Fall, (e)s, ¨e	fall; *also* case[1]
der Schaden, s, ¨-	harm, damage
wie schade!	what a pity!
beschädigen	to harm

[1] **Auf jeden Fall,** in any case, at any rate; **auf alle Fälle,** at all events, by all means.

21

(sich) weh tun, a, a	to hurt (oneself)
(sich) verwunden	to wound (oneself)
die Wunde, -, n	wound
der Chirurg, en, en	surgeon
(den) Schnupfen haben	to have a cold
sich erkälten	to catch a cold, get cold
kalt	cold
die Kälte, -, ***n.p.***	cold, coldness
husten	to cough
der Husten, s, ***n.p.***	cough

22

heizen	to heat, warm
(er)wärmen	to warm
heiß	hot, warm
warm	warm, hot
die Hitze, -, ***n.p.***	heat
die Wärme, -, ***n.p.***	heat
schwitzen	to sweat, perspire
das Fieber, s, ***n.p.***	fever; *also* temperature[1]
ansteckend	contagious, infectious
der Narr, en, en	madman, fool

23

verrückt	mad, crazy
die Torheit, -, en	folly
töricht	foolish, stupid
albern	silly
dumm	stupid
die Dummheit, -, en	stupidity
der Tod,[2] (e)s	death
der Tote, n, n	dead man
tot	dead
töten	to kill

[1] Fieber haben, to have a temperature, to be feverish.

[2] Plural Todesfälle, deaths, casualties.

24

tödlich	mortal, deadly
sterben,† a, o, i	to die
(un)sterblich	(im)mortal
die Leiche, -, n	corpse
der Sarg, (e)s, ¨ e	coffin
das Grab, (e)s, ¨ er	grave, tomb
(be)graben, u, a, ä	to dig (bury)
das Begräbnis, ses, se	funeral
die Trauer, -, *n.p.*	mourning
in Trauer sein (um)	to be in mourning (for)

DIE FAMILIE—THE FAMILY

25

die Verwandtschaft, -, en	relationship, relatives
der (die) Verwandte, n, n	relation
verwandt (mit)	related (to)
der Vorfahr, en, en	ancestor
der Nachkomme, n, n	descendant
die Eltern, *pl.*	parents
die Großeltern	grandparents
der Vater, s, ¨ -	father
die Mutter, -, ¨-	mother
die Großmutter	grandmother

26

lieben	to love
die Liebe, -, *n.p.*	love, affection; charity
gern haben	to like, be fond of
lieb	dear
liebevoll	affectionate
liebenswürdig	amiable, lovable
küssen	to kiss
der Kuß, (ss)es, ¨(ss)e	kiss
die Heirat, -, en	marriage
die Hochzeit, -, en	wedding

27

der Mann, (e)s, ¨er	man; *also* husband
die Frau, -, en	woman, lady; wife
die Braut, -, ¨e	fiancée; *also* bride
der Bräutigam, s, e	fiancé; *also* bridegroom
der Sohn, (e)s, ¨e	son
die Tochter, -, ¨-	daughter
der Enkel, s, -	grandson
die Enkelin, -, nen	granddaughter
der Bruder, s, ¨-	brother
die Schwester, -, n	sister

28

die Geschwister, *pl.*	brothers and/or sisters
der Schwager, s, ¨-	brother-in-law
die Schwägerin, -, nen	sister-in-law
der Schwiegervater	father-in-law
der Schwiegersohn	son-in-law
der Onkel, s, -	uncle
die Tante, -, n	aunt
der Neffe, n, n	nephew
die Nichte, -, n	niece
der Vetter, s, n	cousin

29

die Cousine, -, n	cousin (*f.*)
die Base, -, n	cousin (*f.*)
das Alter, s, -	age, old age
geboren werden, u, o, i	to be born
die Geburt, -, en	birth
das Leben, s, -	life
leben	to live
erziehen, o, o	to bring up, educate
ungezogen	ill-bred
ermahnen	to admonish, exhort

30

das Kind, (e)s, er child
kindlich childlike, filial
die Kindheit childhood
der Knabe, n, n boy
das (junge) Mädchen, s, - girl (young lady)
das Kindermädchen nurse, nanny
der *or* ein Junge, n, n[1] boy, lad
die Jugend, -, ***n.p.*** youth
der Jüngling, (e)s, e young man, youth
(das) Fräulein, s, - miss; *also* (tel.) operator, shop assistant, home governess

31

jung young
(auf-)wachsen,† u, a, ä to grow (grow up)
zu-nehmen, a, o, i to increase (*intr.*)
der Diener, s, - servant
das Dienstmädchen, s, - housemaid
die Magd, -, ¨e housemaid
(be)dienen ***dat.*** **(*****acc.*****)** to serve
in Dienst treten, a, e, i to take service
der Mensch, en, en man; human being
das Weib, es, er woman; female

32

die Dame, -, n lady
der Herr, n, en gentleman; master
die Herrin, -, nen mistress
der Greis, es, e old man
alt (werden, u, o, i) old, aged (to grow old)
die Zeit, -, en time
die Gegenwart, -, ***n.p.*** the present
die Vergangenheit, -, ***n.p.*** the past
die Zukunft, -, ***n.p.*** the future
gegenwärtig present

[1] Colloquial plural **Jungens.**

33

vergehen,† i, a	to pass, elapse, vanish
vergänglich	fleeting
zukünftig	future
an-fangen, i, a, ä	to begin
beginnen, a, o	to begin
der Anfang, (e)s, ¨e	beginning
(be)endigen	to end (finish, *tr.*)
das Ende, s, n	end
(un)endlich	final (endless, infinite)
vollendet	ended, finished

34

folgen,† *dat.*	to follow; obey
folgen,† (auf *a.***)**	to succeed, come after
die Folge, -, n	succession, continuation,
erlauben	to permit, allow [result
um Erlaubnis bitten, a, e	to ask leave *or* permis-
der Augenblick, (e)s, e	moment [sion
die Sekunde, -, n	second
die Minute, -, n	minute
die Stunde, -, n	hour; lesson
die Uhr,[1] -, en	watch, clock; o'clock

35

die Viertelstunde	quarter of an hour
die halbe Stunde	half an hour
vor-gehen,† i, a	to be fast
nach-gehen,† i, a	to be slow
(all)täglich	daily (everyday [*adj.*])
der Tag, es, e	day
der Geburtstag, (e)s, e	birthday
der Feiertag	holiday, any Sunday
der Arbeits- *or* **Werktag**	working day, weekday
heute	today

[1] **Um wieviel Uhr?** At what time? **Um drei Uhr,** at 3 o'clock.

36

(vor)gestern	(the day before) yester-[day
(über)morgen	(the day after) tomorrow
der Morgen, s, -	morning
früh	early
hell	clear, bright
die Helligkeit, -, en	clearness, brightness
die Dunkelheit, -, en	darkness
der Mittag, s, e	noon, midday
der Vor-, Nachmittag	forenoon, afternoon
spät	late

37

(sich) verspäten	to delay (to be *or* come [late)
die Nacht, -, ¨e	night
die Mitternacht	midnight
die Woche, -, n	week
wöchentlich	weekly
der Monat, s, e	month
monatlich	monthly
das (Schalt)Jahr, (e)s, e	(leap) year
das Vierteljahr	quarter
jährlich	yearly

38

die Jahreszeit, -, en	season
das Jahrzehnt, s, e	decade
das Jahrhundert, s, e	century
ewig	eternal
die Ewigkeit, -	eternity
dauern	to last
die Dauer, -, *n.p.*	duration
dauerhaft	lasting
der Kalender, s, -	calendar
das Datum, s, -ten[1]	date

[1]Also plural **Data.**

DAS HAUS—THE HOUSE

39

der Haushalt, (e)s, e	household
die Haushälterin, -, nen	housekeeper
das Haushaltsgeld, (e)s, er	housekeeping money [or allowance
(ver)mieten	to rent (let)
der Mieter, s, -	tenant
die Miete, -, n	rent
um-ziehen,† o, o	to move into another [house
der Besitzer, s, -	landlord, owner
besitzen, a, e	to own, possess
der Besitz, es, *n.p.*	possession

40

gehören	to belong
die Wohnung, -, en	house, dwelling
der Bewohner, s, -	inhabitant
(be)wohnen	to live, stay (inhabit)
das Wochenendhaus, es, ¨er	weekend house
die Hütte, -, n	cottage
der Palast, (e)s, ¨e	palace
die Burg, -, en	castle
der (Kirch)Turm, (e)s, ¨e	tower (steeple)
das Gebäude, s, -	building

41

bauen	to build; *also* till, grow [(*plants*)
fest	strong, firm
zerstören	to destroy
reparieren	to repair
der Plan, (e)s, ¨e	plan
der Architekt, en, en	architect
der Grund, (e)s, ¨e	ground, bottom
gründen	to found, establish
der (Bau)Stein, (e)s, e	(building) stone
der Ziegel(stein)	brick

42

der Sand, es, *n.p.*	sand
die Mauer, -, n	wall (*outside*)
die Wand, -, ¨e	wall (*inside*)
der Maurer, s, -	mason, bricklayer
der Mörtel, s, *n.p.*	mortar
der Zement, (e)s, e	cement
der Gips, es, e	plaster
das Brett, (e)s, er	board, plank
der Balken, s, -	beam
stützen	to support, stay (*tr.*)

43

das Äußere, n, *n.p.*	outside, exterior
das Innere, n, *n.p.*	inside, interior
enthalten, ie, a, ä	to contain
das Fenster, s, -	window
der Balkon, s, s[1]	balcony
die (Fenster)Scheibe, -, n	window-pane
das Glas, es, ¨er	glass (*also for drinking*)
der Vorhang, (e)s, ¨e	curtain
die Tür, -, en	door
das Tor,[2] **(e)s, e**	gate, carriage entrance

44

an-klopfen	to knock
der Eingang, (e)s, ¨e	entrance
öffnen	to open
auf-machen	to open
zu-machen	to close, shut
die Öffnung, -, en	opening
ein-treten,† a, e, i	to enter, step into
aus-gehen,† i, a	to go out
der Ausgang, (e)s, ¨e	exit, way out
das Schloß, (ss)es, ¨(ss)er	lock; *also* castle

[1] Plural also Balkone. [2] Cf. groups 382 and 383.

45

der Schlosser, s, -	locksmith, fitter, mecha-
der Schlüssel, s, -	key [nic
(ver)schließen, o, o	to close, lock, shut up
der Schluß, (ss)es, ¨(ss)e	end, conclusion
die Glocke, -, n	bell
die Klingel, -, n	(small) bell
klingeln	to ring
die Treppe, -, n	stairs, staircase
das Geländer, s, -	banisters; *also* balustrade
die Leiter,[1] -, n	ladder, (house) steps

46

der Aufzug, (e)s, ¨e	lift; *also* act (*drama*)
das Stockwerk, s, e	storeys (*pl.*)
das Erdgeschoß, (ss)es, (ss)e	ground floor
erster Stock	first floor
der Keller, s, -	cellar
der Kellner, s, -	waiter
das Dach, (e)s, ¨er	roof
der Schornstein, (e)s, e	chimney
der (Dach)Ziegel, s, -	(roof) tile
die Kachel, -, n	(*wall or floor*) tile

47

die Decke, -, n	ceiling; *also* cover
bedecken	to cover
der Boden, s, ¨-	ground; *also* loft
der Fußboden	floor; ground
(sich) drehen	to turn (oneself)
(sich) wenden,[2] a, a	to turn
der (Back)Ofen, s, ¨-	stove (oven)
der Kamin, (e)s, e	chimney; fireplace, fire-
das Feuer, s, -	fire [side
der Funke, n(s), n	spark

[1] Cf. leiten in group 83. [2] Also regular.

48

die Feuerversicherung, -, en	fire insurance
die Asche, -, n	ashes
der Rauch, (e)s, *n.p.*	smoke
rauchen	to smoke
brennen, a, a	to burn
glühend	glowing, burning
die Glut, -, en	glow, blaze
die Kohle, -, n	coal
die Holzkohle	charcoal
das (Brenn)Holz, es, ¨er	wood (firewood)

49

das Streichholz, es, ¨er	match
die (Zentral)Heizung, -, en	(central) heating
an-zünden	to light (*fire, lamp*)
an-stecken	to light, set alight
der Brand,[1] (e)s, ¨e	fire, conflagration
die Schachtel, -, n	box
die Beleuchtung, -, en	lighting, illumination
das Licht, (e)s, er	light
(er)leuchten	to light, shine (light up, illuminate)
an-machen (aus-—)	to light (to put out)

50

die Lampe, -, n	lamp
die Laterne, -, n	lantern; street lamp
der Schatten, s, -	shadow, shade
schattig	shady
die Kerze, -, n	candle
das Zimmer, s, -	room
die Stube, -, n	room
der Saal, (e)s, Säle	hall, large room
das Möbel,[2] s, -	piece of furniture
(un)möbliert	(un)furnished

1 **In Brand stecken**, to set fire to *or* on fire.
2 Cf. **das Mobiliar, s, *n.p.***, the furniture.

51

der Flur, es, e	vestibule, (entrance) hall
der Haken, s, -	hook; peg; clasp
der (Regen)Mantel, s, ¨-	(rain)coat
die imprägnierte Kleidung	waterproof clothing
wasserdicht	waterproof (*adj.*)
(be)schützen (vor *d.*)	to protect (from)
der Schutz, es, *n.p.*	shelter; protection
der Hut, (e)s, ¨e	hat
die Mütze, -, n	cap
der Stock, es, ¨e	(walking) stick

52

der Salon, s, s	drawing-room
das Wohnzimmer, s, -	sitting- *or* living-room
der Gast, (e)s, ¨e	guest; visitor
der Gastgeber, s, -	host
die Einladung, -, en	invitation
ein-laden, u, a, ä	to invite
der Stuhl, (e)s, ¨e	chair
die Lehne, -, n	back, support
sitzen, a, e	to sit, be seated; fit (*of clothes*)
(sich) setzen	to place (sit down)

53

der Sitz, es, e	seat
der Sessel, s, -	arm- *or* easy-chair
der Schrank, (e)s, ¨e	cupboard, cabinet
das Sofa, s, s	sofa, couch
(un)bequem	(un)comfortable, (in)convenient
gemütlich	cosy, cheery
die Bank, -, ¨e[1]	bench, seat, form
das Buch, (e)s, ¨er	book
der Bücherschrank	bookcase
die Bücherei, -, en	library

[1] **Cf. die Bank, -, en, in group 253.**

54

der Schreibtisch, (e)s, e	writing-table *or* desk
(be)schreiben, ie, ie	to write (describe)
der Teppich, s, e	carpet, rug
die Tapete, -, n	wallpaper
der Tapezierer, s, -	upholsterer,paperhanger
hängen (an *d.*)	to hang (from)
ab-hängen	to take down
auf-hängen	to hang up
das Bild, es, er	picture, image
bilden	to form, make

55

sich (*dat.*) ein-bilden	to imagine
das Bildnis, ses, se	portrait, image
der Rahmen, s, -	frame
das Eßzimmer, s, -	dining-room
essen, a, e, i	to eat
speisen	to eat, dine
die Mahlzeit, -, en	meal
das Frühstück, s, e	breakfast
frühstücken	to breakfast
das Mittagessen, s, -	lunch *or* dinner

56

das Abendessen, s, -	evening meal *or* supper
die (Unter)Tasse, -, n	cup (saucer)
der Kaffee, s, *n.p.*	coffee
der Tee, s, *n.p.*	tea
die Teekanne, -, n	teapot
der Kakao, s, *n.p.*	cocoa
die Schokolade, -, *n.p.*	chocolate
der Zucker, s, *n.p.*	sugar
süß	sweet
bitter	bitter

57

das Tablett, s, e	tray
die Milch, -, *n.p.*	milk
die Molkerei, -, en	dairy
die Sahne, -, *n.p.*	cream
der Rahm, (e)s, *n.p.*	skin (*milk*); cream
die Butter, -, *n.p.*	butter
das Brot, (e)s, e	bread
der Laib, (e)s, e	loaf
das Brötchen, s, -	roll
das belegte Brot	sandwich

58

eine Schnitte, -, n	a cut, slice, piece (*bread*)
schneiden, i, i	to cut
weich	soft
hart	hard, stale
die Kruste,[1] -, n	crust
der Tisch, (e)s, e	table
das Tischtuch, (e)s, ¨er	tablecloth
die Serviette, -, n	napkin
die Anrichte, -, n	sideboard
die Schublade, -, n	drawer

59

(an-)bieten, o, o	to offer
reichen	to reach; *also* hand, pass
der Teller, s, -	plate
die Schüssel, -, n	dish
der Deckel, s, -	lid
zu-decken	to cover
(ab-)decken	to lay [*the table*] (to clear)
entdecken	to discover
das (Tafel)Besteck, (e)s, e	knife, fork and spoon
(zer)brechen, a, o, i	to break

[1] Also die (Brot)Rinde, crust (of bread).

60

der Löffel, s, -	spoon
die Gabel, -, n	fork
das Messer, s, -	knife
scharf	sharp
stumpf	blunt
kurz	short
lang	long
langsam	slow
schnell	quick
die Flasche, -, n	bottle, flask

61

der Kork, (e)s, e	cork
der Korkzieher, s, -	corkscrew
(er†)trinken, a, u	to drink (drown)
das Getränk, (e)s, e	beverage, drink
das Bier, (e)s, e	beer, ale
der Wein, (e)s, e	wine
das (Trink)Wasser, s, *n.p.*	(drinking) water
trüb	muddy (*of water*); dim, gloomy
(un)rein	(un)clean
das Gefäß,[1] **es, e**	vessel; *also* hilt (*sword*)

62

der Alkohol, s, *n.p.*	spirit
die Lebensmittel, *pl.*	provisions, victuals, [groceries
(er)nähren[2]	to nourish, feed (support, maintain)
der Hunger, s, *n.p.*	hunger
hungrig	hungry
(ver†)hungern	to be hungry (die of hunger)
der Durst, (e)s, *n.p.*	thirst
die Suppe, -, n	soup, broth
das Rindfleisch, (e)s, *n.p.*	beef
das Hammelfleisch	mutton

[1] See also group 352. [2] Cf. **unterstützen** in group 260.

63

zart	tender, soft
zäh(e)	tough
die Sauce, -, n	sauce, gravy
das Kotelett, s, s	chop, cutlet
der Schinken, s, -	ham
der Speck, (e)s, *n.p.*	bacon
die Wurst, -, ¨e	sausage
der Eierkuchen, s, -	omelette, pancake
das Gemüse, s, -	vegetables
der Reis, es, *n.p.*	rice

64

der Salat, (e)s, e	salad, lettuce
das Öl, (e)s, e	oil
der Essig, s, *n.p.*	vinegar
sauer	sour
das Sauerkraut, s, *n.p.*	pickled cabbage
das Salz, es, e	salt
der Pfeffer, s, *n.p.*	pepper
der Senf, s, *n.p.*	mustard
begehren	to desire, wish for; covet
gierig	greedy; eager

65

die Gier, -, *n.p.*	eagerness; greed
der Nachtisch, s, *n.p.*	dessert
der Käse, s, -	cheese
die (Orangen)Marmelade, -, n	jam (marmalade)
das (Apfel)Mus, es, e	jam (stewed apples)
der (Apfel)Kuchen, s, -	cake (apple tart)
die Pastete, -, n	pie, pastry
der Teig, (e)s, e	dough, paste
der Konditor, s, en	pastrycook, confectioner
die Konditorei, -, en	confectioner's shop

66

backen, u, a, ä	to bake
der Bäcker, s, -	baker
die Bäckerei, -, en	bakehouse, baker's shop
die Torte, -, n	tart
das Keks, es, - *or* **e**	biscuit
der Zwieback, s, e	rusk, biscuit
wohlschmeckend	very nice *or* tasty
vortrefflich	excellent
die Küche, -, n	kitchen; cooking
kochen	to cook

67

die Köchin, -, nen	cook
der Koch, s, ¨e	cook, chef
roh	raw
der (Küchen)Herd, (e)s, e	hearth (kitchen range)
das Gulasch,[1] es, *n.p.*	a stew of minced meat (*with bacon, onions, pepper etc.*)
der Braten, s, -	roast meat; joint
braten, ie, a, ä	to roast, fry
die Bratkartoffeln, *f. pl.*	fried potatoes
die (Brat)Pfanne, -, n	frying-pan
das Gerät, (e)s, e	utensil

68

das (Küchen)Geschirr, (e)s, e	crockery, plates, [dishes, china, etc.
der Topf, es, ¨e	pot
der Kessel, s, -	kettle; *also* cauldron, boiler
der Eimer, s, -	pail, bucket
(aus-)gießen, o, o	to pour (pour out)
der Korb, (e)s, ¨e	basket
(er)füllen	to fill (fulfil)
voll	full
leer	empty
leeren	to empty, clear (out)

[1] In spite of all dictionaries everybody says der Gulasch.

69

der Besen, s, -	sweeping-brush, broom
kehren	to sweep
fegen	to sweep
spülen	to wash up, rinse
der Hahn, (e)s, ¨e	tap; *also* cock
das Schlafzimmer, s, -	bedroom
(ein-†)schlafen, ie, a, ä	to sleep (fall asleep)
auf-wachen†	to awake (*intr.*)
(auf-)wecken	to awake (*tr.*)
der Wecker, s, -	alarm clock

70

der Schlaf, (e)s, *n.p.*	sleep, doze
der Traum, (e)s, ¨e	dream
träumen (von)	to dream (dream of *s.th.*)
liegen, a, e	to lie (down)
legen	to lay, put
das Bett, (e)s, en	bed
das Zimmermädchen, s, -	maid (*in hotel*)
der Staub, (e)s, *n.p.*	dust
das Staubtuch, (e)s, ¨er	duster
ab-wischen	to wipe

71

helfen, a, o, i (*dat.*)	to help
die Hilfe,[1] -, *n.p.*	help, assistance
die Matratze, -, n	mattress
das Bettuch, (e)s, ¨er	sheet
das Kissen, s, -	pillow, cushion
die Bettdecke, -, n	blanket, coverlet
die Matte, -, n	rug, mat
auf-stehen,† a, a	to get up, rise
(sich er)heben, o, o	to raise, lift (rise)
das Kleid, (e)s, er	dress, garment

[1] die erste Hilfe, first aid.

72

(sich) an-ziehen, o, o	to put on (dress)
(sich) aus-ziehen, o, o	to take off (undress)
auf-setzen	to put on (*a hat*)
der Kleiderschrank, (e)s, ¨e	wardrobe
die Wäsche, -, *n.p.*	washing, linen, clothes
waschen, u, a, ä	to wash
die Wäscherin, -, nen	washerwoman, laundress
das Leinen, s, -	linen, linen goods
das Tuch, (e)s, ¨er	cloth
grob	coarse

73

die (Kunst)Seide, -, n	(artificial) silk
seidig	silky
das Hemd, (e)s, en	shirt; chemise
die Krawatte, -, n	neck-tie
der Anzug, (e)s, ¨e	suit of clothes
der Schneider, s, -	tailor
die Schneiderin, -, nen	dressmaker
neu	new, modern
schmal	narrow
elegant	elegant, graceful

74

eng	narrow, tight
weit	broad, wide
fertig	finished; *also* ready *and* ready to wear
verfertigen	to make
machen lassen, ie, a, ä	to get made *or* have done[1]
bestellen	to order (*goods*); *also* book (*seats*)
die Bestellung, -, en	order
bringen, a, a	to bring
nützlich	useful
nutzlos	useless

[1] **Er läßt ein Haus bauen,** he has a house built; **ich werde es reparieren lassen,** I shall have it repaired.

75

die Jacke, -, n	jacket (*man's or woman's*)
der Rock, (e)s, ¨e	jacket (*man's*); *also* skirt
die Weste, -, n	waistcoat
die Hose,-, n	trousers
die Unterhose, -, n	pants, drawers
die Socke, -, n	sock
der Strumpf, (e)s, ¨e	stocking
stopfen	to darn
flicken	to patch, mend
der Schuhmacher, s, -	shoemaker

76

der Schuh, (e)s, e	shoe, boot
der Stiefel, s, -	(knee) boot
die Bluse, -, n	blouse
der Gürtel, s, -	belt, girdle
die Schürze, -, n	apron
das Halstuch, (e)s, ¨er	scarf
der Kragen, s, -	collar
der Ärmel, s, -	sleeve
der Handschuh, s, e	glove
der Knopf, (e)s, ¨e	button; stud; knob

77

nähen	to sew
die Näherei, -, en	sewing
die Stickerei, -, en	embroidery
der Faden, s, ¨-	thread
die (Steck)Nadel, -, n	needle (pin)
stecken	to stick, fix
die Schere, -, n	scissors
das Band, (e)s, ¨er	ribbon, tape, band
(los-)binden, a, u	to bind, (un)tie
die Schnur, -, ¨e	string, cord, twine; *also* string of beads

78

der Schleier, s, -	veil
die Spitzen, ***pl.***	lace
(un)modern	in fashion (out of —)
die Mode, -, n	fashion
die Modistin, -, nen	milliner
das Modewarengeschäft, (e)s, e	milliner's shop
die Modewaren ***f. pl.***	novelties, fancy goods
der Putz, es, ***n.p.***	millinery, finery
das Kostüm, s, e	costume, fancy dress; [*also* two-piece
die Tasche, -, n	pocket

79

das Taschentuch, (e)s, ¨er	handkerchief
die Handtasche, -, n	handbag
das Portemonnaie, s, s	purse
das Badezimmer, s, -	bathroom
das Bad, (e)s, ¨er	bath
die Badewanne, -, n	bath, bathing-tub
baden	to bathe
das Handtuch, (e)s, ¨er	towel
sauber	clean, neat
schmutzig	dirty

80

der Waschtisch, (e)s, e	washstand
der Spiegel, s, -	mirror
das Waschbecken, s, -	basin
die Kanne, -, n	jug
der Schwamm, (e)s, ¨e	sponge
die Seife, -, n	soap
der Kamm, (e)s, ¨e	comb
kämmen	to comb
die Bürste, -, n	(clothes) brush
bürsten	to brush

81

die Zahnbürste, -, n	toothbrush
der Puder, s, ***n.p.***	(face) powder
der Schmuck, (e)s, ***n.p.***	adornment, jewels
zieren	to adorn
die Brosche, -, n	brooch
das Halsband, (e)s, ¨er	necklace; *also* collar (*for dogs*)
das Armband	bracelet
der (Ohr)Ring, (e)s, e	ring (earring)
die Gabe, -, n	gift
geben, a, e, i	to give

ERZIEHUNG UND UNTERRICHT —GENERAL EDUCATION

82

öffentlich	public
der (Privat)Unterricht, (es,) ***n.p.***	(private) tuition
unterrichten	to teach, educate
die Volksschule, -, n	primary school
die Mittelschule, -, n	intermediate school
die höhere Schule	secondary school
die Hochschule, -, n	university
das Gymnasium, s, -sien	classical college *or* grammar school
der Direktor, s, en	principal, headmaster; *also* manager
die Direktorin, -, nen	headmistress

83

die Erziehung, -, en	upbringing, education
leiten	to lead, guide
die Leitung, -, en	direction, guidance
lehren	to teach
der Lehrgang, (e)s, ¨e (in ***d.*****)**	the course (of)
gelehrt	learned
der Lehrer, s, - (-in)	teacher (lady teacher)
der Professor, s, en	professor
gebildet	educated, cultured
die Universität, -, en	university

84

die Klasse, -, n	class
der Schüler, s, - (-in)	pupil (girl pupil)
der Schulkamerad, en, en	schoolmate
(auswendig) lernen	to learn (by heart)
studieren	to study
der Student, en, en	student
der Platz, es, ¨ e	place, seat
die Tafel, -, n	blackboard
die Kreide, -, n	chalk
der Bleistift, (e)s, e	pencil

85

die Tinte, -, n	ink
das Tintenfaß, (ss)es, ¨ (ss)er	inkwell, inkstand
der Füller, s, -	fountain pen
der Kugelschreiber, s, -	ballpoint pen
das Lineal, s, e	ruler
die Linie, -, n	line
die Zeile, -, n	line (*of a book*)
das Heft, (e)s, e	copy book, writing book
die Seite, -, n	page; *also* side
das Papier, (e)s, e	paper

86

der Bogen Papier	sheet of paper
das Löschblatt, (e)s, ¨ er	blotting-paper
falten	to fold; *also* crease
brauchen	to use; *also* want
gebraucht	second-hand
(be)nutzen[1]	to be of use (make use of)
der Nutzen, s, *n.p.*	use, benefit
bedürfen, u, u, a	to need, be in want of
die Not, -, ¨ e	necessity, want
(un)nötig	(un)necessary

[1] **Wozu nutzt das?** What is the good of it, *or* of that? **Das nützt nichts,** that is not good for anything. **Was nutzt es, daß—?** What avails it, that—?
N.B. This verb has two forms: **(be)nutzen** and **(be)nützen.**

87

die Arbeit, -, en	work [ing
arbeitsam	industrious, hard-work-
(be)arbeiten	to work (work, *tr.*)
der Arbeiter, s, -	worker, workman
fleißig	studious, diligent
eine Stunde geben, a, e, i	to give a lesson
der Stundenplan, (e)s, ¨e	time-table
die Lektion, -, en	lesson (*in a book*)
auf-sagen	to recite; say (*a lesson*)
vergessen, a, e, i	to forget

88

vergeßlich	forgetful
zerstreut sein	to be absent-minded
die Zerstreuung, -, en	absence of mind, distraction
(un)aufmerksam	(in)attentive
auf-passen (auf *a.*)	to be attentive (to)
acht-geben (auf *a.*)	to attend, pay attention (to)
die Achtung, -, *n.p.*	esteem, regard, attention
achten	to esteem, respect
teil-nehmen, a, o, i (an *d.*)	to take part (in)
erklären	to explain

89

die Erklärung, -, en	explanation; declaration
klar	clear
(vor-)lesen, a, e, ie	to read (read to *or* aloud)
die Vorlesung, -, en	lecture
die Lektüre, -, *n.p.*	reading; reading matter
die Aufgabe, -, n	task, problem
die Übung, -, en	exercise, practice
ein-üben	to exercise, drill, study
aus-üben	to practise (*one's profession*)
der Fehler, s, -	error, fault, defect

90

fehlen (*intr.*)	to miss, fail, make a mistake
vermissen	to miss (*tr.*)
anwesend	present
abwesend	absent
leicht	easy; *also* light
schwer	difficult; *also* heavy
die Leichtigkeit, -, *n.p.*	easiness, facility
die Schwierigkeit, -, en	difficulty
der Fortschritt, (e)s, e	improvement, progress
die Pflicht, -, en	duty

91

das Examen, s, -mina	examination
die Prüfung, -, en	test, examination
prüfen	to examine (*exam.*)
bestehen, a, a (aus)	to consist (of); to pass
gelingen,†[1] **a, u** (*imp.*)	to succeed (*in doing*), manage (*to do*)
der Erfolg, (e)s, e	success
(ver)suchen	to seek, look for (try)
tadeln (wegen *g.***)**	to blame (for)
loben (wegen)	to praise (for)
der Tadel, s, -	blame

92

das Lob, (e)s, *n.p.*	praise
billigen	to approve
die Note, -, n	mark; note
korrigieren	to correct
notieren	to note; to write down
das Notizbuch, (e)s, ¨ er	notebook
der Preis, es, e	prize; price
belohnen	to reward
die Belohnung, -, en	reward
die Ferien, *pl.*	holidays

[1] **es gelingt mir,** I succeed *or* prosper in; **die Aufgabe gelingt ihm,** he succeeded in his task; **es gelang mir nicht, meinen Plan auszuführen,** I was not able to carry out my plan; **es ist ihm übel gelungen,** he has had no success, he has failed.

93

das Betragen, s, *n.p.*	conduct, behaviour
(sich) betragen, u, a, ä	to amount to (behave)
die Anstrengung, -, en	effort, endeavour
sich an-strengen	to exert oneself, strive
der Eifer, s, *n.p.*	zeal
eifrig	zealous, eager
eifersüchtig	jealous
die Eifersucht, -, *n.p.*	jealousy
(un)gehorsam	(dis)obedient
träge	lazy

94

faul	lazy
die Faulheit, -, en	laziness
(ver)warnen	to warn (forewarn)
die Warnung, -, en	warning, caution
streng	strict, severe
die Strenge, -, *n.p.*	severity
die Drohung, -, en	threat
drohen (*dat.*)	to threaten
die Strafe, -, n	punishment, penalty
(be)strafen	to punish

95

die Vergebung, -, en	pardon, forgiveness
vergeben, a, e, i	to pardon, forgive
verdienen	to deserve
die Grammatik, -, en	grammar
zeigen	to show, point out
die Rechtschreibung, -, en	spelling
(falsch)buchstabieren	to spell[1] (misspell)
der Buchstabe, n(s), n	letter, type
die Regel, -, n	rule
(un)regelmäßig	(ir)regular

[1] Cf. **Wie schreibt man das?** How do you spell it? **Es schreibt sich mit,** it is spelt with.

96

die Ausnahme, -, n	exception
der Punkt, (e)s, e	point, dot, full stop
eine Frage stellen	to ask a question
fragen (nach)	to ask, inquire (about)
die Bitte, -, n	entreaty, request
bitten, a, e (um)	to entreat, beg
antworten	to reply, answer
die Antwort, -, en	reply, answer
verantwortlich	responsible
aus-rufen, ie, u	to exclaim, call out

97

der Artikel, s, -	article
das Substantiv, s, e	noun, substantive
(er)nennen, a, a	to name (appoint)
heißen, ie, ei	to be called
der (Vor)Name, ns, n	(Christian *or* first) name
sich beziehen, o, o (auf *a.*)	to refer (to)
der Satz, es, ¨ e	sentence (*gram.*)
die Satzlehre, -, n	syntax
das Wort, (e)s, ¨ er[1]	word
das Wörterbuch, (e)s, ¨ er	dictionary

98

das Sprichwort, (e)s, ¨ er	proverb, saying
der Ausdruck, (e)s, ¨ e	expression
ausdrucksvoll	expressive
(aus-)drücken[2]	to press, squeeze (express)
der Eindruck, (e)s, ¨ e	impression
die Handschrift, -, en	handwriting
die Abschrift, -, en	copy
der Redner, s, -	orator, speaker
die Beredsamkeit, -, *n.p.*	eloquence
sich unterhalten, ie, a, ä	to converse

[1] Also plural Worte; means then 'expressions, speech'.
[2] Cf. drucken in group 104.

99

die Unterhaltung, -, en	conversation; *also* entertainment
unterhaltend	entertaining, amusing
das Gespräch, (e)s, e	dialogue, conversation
ein Gespräch führen	to carry on a conversation
das Beispiel, s, e	example
die Bedeutung, -, en	sense, meaning
bedeuten	to mean
(un)deutlich	clear, (in)distinct
die Übersetzung, -, en	translation
übersetzen	to translate

100

der Dolmetscher, s, -	interpreter
die Literatur, -, en	literature
die Dichtung, -, en	fiction; *also* poetry
die Lyrik, -, *n.p.*	lyric poetry
der Dichter, s, - (-in)	poet (poetess); writer (*of fiction*)
der Schriftsteller, s, -	writer, author
zitieren	to quote
das Zitat, (e)s, e	quotation
der Stil, (e)s, e	style
der Verfasser, s, -	author, writer

101

verwirren[1]	to entangle, confuse
die Verwirrung, -, en	confusion
vor-stellen	to represent, mean; introduce (*a person*)
stellen	to place, put
her-stellen	to restore
die Stelle, -, n	place; *also* situation
die Phantasie, -, n	fancy, imagination
die Idee, -, n	idea, notion
entwickeln	to develop, unfold
die Entwicklung, -, en	development, evolution

[1] Past part. verworren, when used as an adjective.

102

der Zweck, (e)s, e	aim, object
die Erzählung, -, en	narrative, story
erzählen	to relate, tell
das Märchen, s, -	fairy tale
der Reim, (e)s, e	rhyme
das Gedicht, (e)s, e	poem, verses
das Lied, (e)s, er	song; hymn
die Fabel, -, n	fable
das Drama, s, -men	drama
das Lustspiel, (e)s, e	comedy

103

das Trauerspiel, (e)s, e	tragedy
komisch	comic(al), funny
lustig	merry, jovial
der Roman, (e)s, e	novel
die Novelle, -, n	short novel
der Abschnitt, (e)s, e	part, section; sector
aufregend	exciting
interessieren	to interest
interessant	interesting
die Ausgabe, -, n	edition

104

der Herausgeber, s, -	publisher, editor
heraus-geben, a, e, i	to publish
der Redakteur, s, e	editor (*newspaper*)
drucken	to print
der Drucker, s, -	printer [*also* pressure
der Druck, (e)s, e	print, impression, type;
die (Buch)Druckerei, -, en	printing works, —press,
die Zeitung, -, en	newspaper [—office
der Journalist, en, en	journalist
die Zeitschrift, -, en	review, magazine

105

die Nachricht, -, en	news
benachrichtigen	to inform
an-zeigen	to advertise, bring to notice
die Anzeige, -, n	advertisement
die Reklame, -, n	puffing advertisement
die Geschichte, -, n	history, story
der Historiker, s, -	historian
die Antike, -, *n.p.*	antiquity
die Alten, *pl.*	the ancients
das Mittelalter, s, *n.p.*	Middle Ages

106

der Kreuzzug, (e)s, ¨e	crusade
die Neuzeit, -, *n.p.*	modern times
die Kultur, -, en	civilization; *also* cultivation
das Ereignis, ses, se	event
sich ereignen	to take place, happen
vor-kommen,† a, o	to happen, occur
die Handlung, -, en	action; *also* trade, business
die Tat, -, en	deed, act, action
die Tatsache, -, n	fact
tätig	active

107

die Tätigkeit, -, en	activity
die Ursache, -, n	cause
die Wirkung, -, en	effect
die Freiheit, -, en	liberty, freedom
frei	free
befreien	to free, deliver
das Schicksal, s, e	fate, destiny
die Gewalt, -, en	force, violence, power
die Macht,[1] -, ¨e	might, power
mächtig	mighty, powerful

[1] See also **die Großmächte** in group 362.

108

(un)möglich	(im)possible
das Bündnis, ses, se	alliance
der Bund, es, ¨e	league, union
(sich) verbünden	to ally (themselves)
vergrößern	to increase, enlarge
vermehren	to augment
vermindern	to diminish
der Niedergang, (e)s, ¨e	decline, downfall
die Eroberung, -, en	conquest
erobern	to conquer

109

berühmt	celebrated, renowned
der Ruhm, es, *n.p.*	glory, fame
der Aufruhr, (e)s, e	insurrection, rebellion
aus-wandern†	to emigrate
ein-wandern†	to immigrate
die Geographie, -, *n.p.*	geography
die Karte, -, n	map, chart
erforschen	to explore
der (Nord)Pol, (e)s, e	(north) pole
Süd	south

110

Ost und West	east and west
der Kompaß, (ss)es, (ss)e	compass
die Lage, -, n	position, situation
erreichen	to reach; attain
fern	distant
nah	near
(sich) entfernen	to remove (go away)
(sich) nähern	to bring near (approach)
der Nachbar, n, n	neighbour
an-grenzen	to border upon, adjoin

111

die Grenze, -, n	boundary, frontier
die Kolonie, -, n	colony
das Gebiet, (e)s, e	territory, district
die Gegend, -, en	region, part, country
das Land, es, ¨er	land; country (*nation*)
ländlich	rustic, rural
der Landsmann, (e)s, [*pl.*-leute	compatriot, fellow-coun- [tryman
die (Land)Bevölkerung	(rural) population
die Landschaft, -, en	landscape, district
auf dem Lande	in the country

112

die (Haupt)Stadt, -, ¨e	town (capital)
der Städter, s, -	citizen, townsman
das Volk, (e)s, ¨er	people, nation
die Vereinten Nationen	the United Nations[1]
das Dorf, (e)s, ¨er	village
die Leute, *pl.*	people (*persons*)
der Ort, (e)s, e	place
das Ausland, (e)s, *n.p.*	foreign country
der Ausländer, s, -	foreigner
ausländisch	foreign, exotic

In the four following groups of countries, only the masculines of the inhabitants are given after the adjectives. Just remember that the feminines are formed simply by changing masc. **e** endings to **in**, or adding **in** to those ending in **er** or **ier**. However, note that **Sachse** becomes **Sächsin, Franzose Französin,** and that for 'German' the adjective is used, thus: **der, die, Deutsche, ein Deutscher, eine Deutsche, die Deutschen,** etc.

Note also that most names of countries are neuter, and only require **das** when preceded by an adjective, as **das sonnige Spanien,** sunny Spain.

[1] The United Nations (U.N.O.) superseded in 1945 the former League of Nations, **der Völkerbund,** created in 1919.

113

Europe	Europa	-päisch	Europäer
Germany	Deutschland	deutsch	Deutscher
Prussia	Preußen	-ßisch	Preuße
Saxony	Sachsen	-¨ sisch	Sachse
Bavaria	Bayern	bayrisch	Bayer
Austria	Österreich	-reichisch	-reicher
Gt. Britain	Groß-britannien	britisch	Brite
England	England	-glisch	-gländer
Wales	Wales[1]	Walisisch	Waliser
Scotland	Schottland	schottisch	Schotte

114

Ireland	Irland	irisch	Irländer
France	Frankreich	französisch	Franzose
Netherlands	die Nieder-lande	-ländisch	-länder
Holland	Holland	-ländisch	-länder
Denmark	Dänemark	dänisch	Däne
Sweden	Schweden	-disch	Schwede
Norway	Norwegen	-gisch	-weger
Belgium	Belgien	-gisch	-gier
Switzerland	die Schweiz	-zerisch	-zer
Italy	Italien	-nisch	-ner

115

Spain	Spanien	spanisch	-nier
Portugal	Portugal	-giesisch	-giese
Greece	Griechenland	griechisch	Grieche
Russia	Rußland	russisch	Russe
Turkey	die Türkei	-kisch	Türke
Asia	Asien	asiatisch	Asiate
Arabia	Arabien	-bisch	Araber
China	China	chinesisch	Chinese
Japan	Japan	-panisch	Japaner
India	Indien	indisch	Indier[2]

[1] Pronounced as in English. [2] Indianer is American Indian.

116

Persia	**Persien**	**persisch**	**Perser**
Africa	**Afrika**	**-kanisch**	**-kaner**
Egypt	**Ägypten**	**-tisch**	**Ägypter**
Australia	**Australien**	**-tralisch**	**-tralier**
Canada	**Kanada**	**-nadisch**	**-nadier**
America	**Amerika**	**-kanisch**	**-kaner**
Brazil	**Brasilien**	**-lianisch**	**-lianer**
Cologne	**Köln**	**kölnisch**	**Kölner**
Munich	**München**	**münchnerisch**	**Münchner**
Vienna	**Wien**	**wienerisch**	**Wiener**

117

die Vereinigten Staaten	United States
die Alpen *f. pl.*	Alps
der Rhein, (e)s	Rhine
die Themse	Thames
der Atlantische Ozean	Atlantic Ocean
das (Mittel)Meer, (e)s, e	(Mediterranean) Sea
der Stille Ozean, (e)s, e	Pacific Ocean
die Nordsee	North Sea
die Ostsee	Baltic
der Kanal, (e)s	English Channel[1]

118

die Rechenkunst, -, *n.p.*	arithmetic
die Mathematik, -, *n.p.*	mathematics
das (Kopf)Rechnen, s	(mental) calculation
zählen (auf *d.***)**	to count (rely upon)
die Zahl, -, en	number
die Nummer, -, n	number (*on doors, tickets, etc.*)
die Null, -, en	nought, zero
die Summe, -, n	sum, amount
addieren	to add up, sum up
subtrahieren	to subtract, deduct

[1] **Also canal, with plural Kanäle.**

119

die Subtraktion, -, en	subtraction
der Rest, (e)s, e	rest, remainder
übrig-bleiben,† ie, ie	to remain
übrig	remaining
multiplizieren	to multiply
dividieren	to divide
teilen	to divide, share
der Teil, (e)s, e	part, portion
der Vorteil	advantage
der Nachteil	disadvantage

120

vorteilhaft	advantageous
nachteilig	disadvantageous, prejudicial
der Bruch, (e)s, ¨e	fraction; *also* fracture
(unter-)brechen, a, o, i	to break (interrupt)
die Hälfte, -, n	the half
halb	half
das Drittel, s, -	the third part
das Viertel, s, -	the quarter, fourth part
das Dutzend, s, e	dozen
doppelt	double

121

dreifach	threefold, triple
einfach	simple
gleich	equal, same, like
die Gleichheit, -, *n.p.*	equality, similarity
der Vergleich, (e)s, e	comparison
vergleichen	to compare
die Geometrie, -, *n.p.*	geometry
die Algebra, -, *n.p.*	algebra
der Raum, (e)s, ¨e	room, space
geräumig	spacious, large

122

die Fläche, -, n	plain, surface; *also* plane
flach	flat, plain, level
senkrecht	vertical, perpendicular
wagrecht	horizontal, level
der (rechte) Winkel, s, -	(right) angle; corner
spitz	acute, pointed
die Ecke, -, n	corner
das Dreieck, (e)s, e	triangle
das Quadrat, (e)s, e	square
das Rechteck, (e)s, e	rectangle

123

viereckig	square
rund	round
gebogen	curved, bent
gerade	straight
der Umfang, (e)s, ¨e	circumference
der Inhalt, (e)s, e	area; *also* contents
der Kreis, es, e	circle
die Mitte, -, n	centre, middle
der Durchmesser, s, -	diameter
die Rechenaufgabe, -, n	(arithmetic) problem

124

(un)genau	(in)accurate, (in)exact
beweisen, ie, ie	to prove, demonstrate
lösen	to solve; *also* loosen
die Lösung, -, en	solution
die Physik, -, *n.p.*	physics
physikalisch	physical
der Stoff, (e)s, e	substance, matter, stuff, material
die Kraft, -, ¨e	force; strength; power
besonder	particular, peculiar
die Bewegung, -, en	movement, motion

125

(sich) bewegen	to move
(un)beweglich	movable (motionless)
die Beschleunigung	hastening, acceleration
die Elektrizität, ***n.p.***	electricity
die Mechanik, -, ***n.p.***	mechanics
erfinden, a, u	to invent
die Optik, -, ***n.p.***	optics
die Linse, -, n	lens; *also* lentil [pulse
zurück-werfen, a, o, i	to reflect (*light*); *also* re-
die Chemie, -, ***n.p.***	chemistry

126

chemisch	chemical
das Laboratorium, s, -rien	laboratory
der Versuch, (e)s, e	attempt, experiment
das Experiment, (e)s, e	experiment
die Mischung, -, en	mixture, compound
mischen	to mix, mingle
die Verbindung, -, en	compound, alliance
zersetzen	to decompose
die Säure, -, n	acid, acidity
die Erfahrung, -, en	experience, practice

127

die Wissenschaft, -, en	science
wissenschaftlich	scientific
das Wissen, s, ***n.p.***	knowledge
die Kenntnis, -, se	knowledge
(er)kennen, a, a	to know, be acquainted with (recognize)
wissen, u, u, ei	to know (=*have learned*)
an-kündigen	to announce, proclaim
sich erkundigen (bei, nach)	to inquire (of, about)
weise	wise
die Weise, -, n	manner, mode

DIE KÜNSTE — THE ARTS

128

die Kunstakademie, -, n art academy *or* school
künstlerisch artistic
künstlich artificial, artful
der Künstler, s, - artist
der Maler, s, - painter
die Malerei, -, en painting
malerisch picturesque
malen to paint
kolorieren to colour
die Ausstellung, -, en exhibition

129

das Museum, s, -seen museum, art gallery
der Führer, s, - guide, leader
führen to lead, guide
die Illustration, -, en illustration
das Urbild, (e)s, er original
das Abbild, (e)s, er copy
nach-bilden to copy
das Gemälde, s, - picture, painting
der Hintergrund, (e)s, ¨e background
die Zeichnung, -, en drawing

130

zeichnen to draw
der Zeichner, s, - draughtsman
der Entwurf, (e)s, ¨e sketch; project
entwerfen, a, o, i to project, draft, sketch
der Umriß, (ss)es, (ss)e outline [out
nach-ahmen to imitate
die Ähnlichkeit, -, en likeness, resemblance
ähnlich resembling, like, similar
der Pinsel, s, - brush (*painting*)
die Staffelei, -, en easel

131

die Farbe, -, n	colour
färben	to colour, dye
die Färberei, -, en	dye-works; dying
farbig	coloured
bunt	variegated, many-coloured
matt	dull
kontrastieren	to contrast (*intr.*)
weiß	white
schwarz; schwärzlich	black; blackish
hellblau[1]	light blue

132

dunkelgrün	dark green
gelb	yellow
braun	brown
rosa[2]	pink
rot; rötlich	red; reddish
lila[2]**; violett**	lilac; violet
purpurn	purple, crimson
grau	grey
mehrere, *pl.*	several
verschieden	different; *pl.* several

133

die Bildhauerei, -, en	sculpture, statuary
der Bildhauer, s, -	sculptor, carver
hauen	to cut (*in stone*)
die Skulptur, -, en	piece of sculpture
die Werkstätte, -, n	workshop
das Werk, (e)s, e	(*produced*) work; *also literary, etc.*
das Vorbild, (e)s, er	model, pattern
die Statue, -, n	statue
das Standbild, (e)s, er	statue
der Gegenstand, (e)s, ¨e	object; subject (*of a picture*)

1 **Berlinerblau,** Prussian blue.
2 Not declined, e.g. **rosa Kleid, lila Band.**

134

die Büste, -, n	bust
die Gruppe, -, n	group
das Denkmal, (e)s, ¨ er	monument, memorial
die Gestalt, -, en	form, figure, shape
gestalten	to form
die Baukunst, -, ¨ e	architecture
der Baumeister, s, -	builder, contractor
unternehmen, a, o, i	to undertake
die Unternehmung, -, en	enterprise
der Kontrakt, (e)s, e	contract

135

der Nachtrag, (e)s, ¨ e	supplement
der Beitrag	contribution
der Vortrag	lecture; (*mus.*) execution
der Auftrag[1]	commission, errand
die Säule, -, n	pillar, column
der Pfeiler, s, -	pillar
das Gewölbe, s, -	vault, arch
die Kuppel, -, n	dome, cupola
das Gerüst, (e)s, e	scaffolding
die Richtung, -, en	direction

136

(auf-)richten	to direct (set upright)
errichten	to erect, set up
ab-schlagen, u, a, ä	to take down; *also* refuse
das Meisterstück, (e)s, e	masterpiece
die Musik, -, *n.p.*	music
musizieren	to play music
die (Musik)Kapelle, -, n	band
der Musiker, s, -	musician
(vom Blatt) spielen	to play (at sight)
der Komponist, en, en	composer

[1] Cf. **einen Auftrag aus-führen,** to execute an order; **—besorgen,** to go a message.

137

die Oper, -, n	grand opera
das Orchester, s, -	orchestra
sanft	soft, gentle, mild
das Streichinstrument	string instrument
das Blasinstrument, s, e	wind instrument
blasen, ie, a, ä	to blow
das Klavier, s, e	piano
der Klavierspieler, s, -	pianist
die Orgel, -, n	organ
die Flöte, -, n	flute

138

der Dudelsack, (e)s, ¨e	bagpipe
das Horn, (e)s, ¨er	cornet
die Trompete, -, n	trumpet
die Violine, -, n	violin, fiddle
die Geige, -, n	violin
der Bogen, s, ¨-	bow; *also* arch
die Saite, -, n	string, chord
die Harfe, -, n	harp
die Trommel, -, n	drum
singen, a, u	to sing

139

der Sänger, s, - (-in)	singer
der Gesang, (e)s, ¨e	song, singing
entzücken	to enchant, charm
der Zauber, s, -	spell, charm
begleiten	to accompany
die Strophe, -, n	strophe, stanza
das Konzert, (e)s, e	concert
der Chor, (e)s, ¨e	chorus; *also* choir
tanzen	to dance
der Tanz, (e)s, ¨e	dance, dancing

140

der Ball, (e)s, ¨e	ball, dance
die Maske, -, n	mask
das Theater, s, -	theatre
besetzt	full; occupied, engaged
die Kasse,[1] -, n	booking-office
eine Eintrittskarte lösen	to buy a ticket
das Parkett, (e)s, e	(orchestra) stalls
das Parterre, s, s	pit
die Loge, -, n	box
hinter der Szene	off stage

141

die Bühne, -, n	stage
die Pause, -, n	interval
die Dekoration, -, en	scenery
das Stück, (e)s, e[2]	play; piece *or* part
die Personen	characters
die Aufführung, -, en	performance
die Truppe, -, n	company
der Zuschauer, s, -	spectator
schauen (auf *a.*)	to look (at)
an-schauen	to look at

142

das Schauspiel, s, e	drama
der Schauspieler, s, - (-in)	actor (actress)
die Rolle, -, n	part
dar-stellen	to (re)present
durch-fallen,† ie, a, ä	to fail, be a failure
der Beifall, s, *n.p.*	applause
(be)klatschen	to clap hands (applaud)
(aus-)pfeifen, i, i	to whistle (hiss [*a play*])
die (Quer)Pfeife, -, n	whistle (fife)
die Vergnügung, -, en	pleasure, amusement

[1] See also group 253.

[2] *n.p.* when meaning *article* or *whole*, not parts of something: 3 Stück Gold, 3 pieces of gold; 10 **Stück Ochsen,** 10 oxen; 15 **Stück Vieh,** 15 head of cattle.

143

sich vergnügen	to enjoy oneself
die Erholung, -, en	relaxation, recreation
sich erholen	to recover (*health*); enjoy oneself
(sich) [er]freuen	to delight (rejoice)
(un)angenehm	(dis)agreeable, (un)pleasant
der Zeitvertreib, s, ***n.p.***	pastime, hobby
müde werden, u, o, i	to get tired
die Müdigkeit, -, en	weariness, lassitude
langweilig	tedious, wearisome
der (Jahr)Markt, (e)s, ¨e	market (fair[1])

144

die Menge, -, n	multitude
belebt	lively; much frequented
der Witz, es, e	wit, joke
der Scherz, es, e	joke, jest
scherzen	to jest, be joking
verspotten	to mock, scoff at, deride
der Spott, (e)s, ***n.p.***	mockery, sneer
der Spaß, es, ¨e	joke, chaff
spaßhaft	jocular, funny
spaßen	to joke

145

lachen	to laugh
das Gelächter, s, ***n.p.***	laugh, laughter
das Lächeln, s, ***n.p.***	smile
lächeln	to smile
der Zigeuner, s, -	gipsy
das Glückspiel, (e)s, e	lottery
das Glück, (e)s, ***n.p.***	fortune, luck
das Unglück, (e)s, ***n.p.***	bad luck
(un)glücklich	(un)lucky, (un)happy, (un)fortunate
der (Ton)Film, (e)s, e	film (talking picture)

[1] Fairground is **der Rummelsplatz** *or* **Vergnügungspark.**

146

das Kino, s, s	cinema
das Spiel, (e)s, e	play, game, match
spielen	to play; gamble
der Spieler, s, -	player; gambler
das Spielfeld, (e)s, er	playing-field, playground
das Spielzeug, (e)s, e	toy, plaything
die Puppe, -, n	doll; *also* chrysalis
gewinnen,[1] a, o	to win
verlieren, o, o	to lose
(sich) täuschen	to deceive (be deceived)

147

betrügen, o, o	to cheat, deceive
trügerisch	deceitful, deceptive
die Gesellschaft, -, en	party; society, company
die Versammlung, -, en	meeting, assembly
(sich) versammeln	to assemble
sich an-schliessen, o, o (*dat. or* an *a.*)	to follow, join
der Besuch, (e)s, e	visit
besuchen	to visit
die Spielkarte, -, n	playing-card
das Billiard, s, s	billiards

148

das Schachspiel, s, e	chess
werfen, a, o, i	to throw, cast
der Würfel, s, -	die, *pl.* dice
das (Kreuzwort)Rätsel, s, -	(crossword) puzzle
raten, ie, a, ä	to guess; advise
im Freien	in the open air
die Hatz, -, en *or* **Hetzjagd**	hunt, chase
die Jagd, -, en	shooting, hunt(ing)
der Jäger, s, -	sportsman, huntsman
jagen	to hunt, shoot (*game*)

See also siegen in groups 230 and 386.

149

schießen,[1] o, o (auf, nach)	to shoot; fire (at)
der Schuß, (ss)es, ¨(ss)e	shot
(sich) verstecken	to hide, conceal (onself)
der Sprung, (e)s, ¨e	leap, jump
springen,‡ a, u	to spring, jump
die Flinte, -, n	gun
die Zielscheibe, -, n	target
das Ziel, (e)s, e	aim, end
zielen (nach; auf *a.*)	to aim at; allude to
der Fischer, s, -	fisher, fisherman

150

fischen	to fish
angeln	to angle, to fish
der Angler, s, -	angler
der Angelhaken, s, -	fishing-hook
das Netz, es, e	net
rudern	to row
das Ruder, s, -	oar
schwimmen,‡ a, o	to swim
retten	to save, rescue
der Liebhaber, s, -	amateur, lover, fancier

151

der Schlitten, s, -	sledge
Schlittschuh (laufen,[2] ie, au, äu)	skate (to skate)
das Rennen, s, -	race
reiten,‡ i, i	to ride
der Reiter, s, -	rider, horseman
die Rennbahn, -, en	racecourse
die Tribüne, -, n	grandstand; *also* platform
die Wette, -, n	bet, wager
wetten	to bet
der (Fuß)Ball, (e)s, ¨e	(foot)ball

[1] See also group 217. [2] **Ich habe Schlittschuh gelaufen, I skated.**

152

das Tennis, -, ***n.p.***	tennis
der Schläger, s, -	racket, bat
(sich) schlagen, u, a, ä	to beat (fight)
das Ringen, s, ***n.p.***	wrestling
das Boxen, s, ***n.p.***	boxing
der Boxer, s, -	boxer
der (Welt)Meister, s, -	(world) champion
das Fechten, s, ***n.p.***	fencing
das Turnen, s, ***n.p.***	gymnastics
der Turner, s, -	gymnast

153

das Auto, s, s	motor car
der Autofahrer, s, -	motorist
fahren,‡ u, a, ä	to go (*in a carriage*), drive
die Spazierfahrt, -, en	drive, sail, row
fort-fahren,† u, a, ä	to continue (*intr.*)
fort-setzen	to continue (*tr.*)
die Fortsetzung, -, en	continuation
das Fahrzeug, (e)s, e	vehicle
das (Fahr)Rad, (e)s, ¨er	wheel (bicycle)
das Motorrad	motor bicycle

154

radeln	to ride a bicycle
der Zeppelin,[1] s, e	airship
der Hubschrauber, s, -	helicopter
der Flieger, s, -	airman; *also* pilot
fliegen,‡ o, o	to fly
das Flugzeug, (e)s, e	aeroplane
die Wanderung, -, en	walking tour
wandern‡	to wander, journey
einen Ausflug machen	to go on an excursion
der Rucksack, (e)s, ¨e	rucksack, knapsack

[1] Named after its inventor, a form of airship (**Luftschiff**) in Germany.

DAS GEISTIGE UND SITTLICHE LEBEN—INTELLECTUAL AND MORAL LIFE

155

der Geist, (e)s, er	mind, spirit, ghost
verstehen, a, a	to understand
der Verstand, (e)s, *n.p.*	understanding, intelligence
verständig	intelligent
(un)verständlich	(un)intelligible
das Mißverständnis, ses, se	misunderstanding
begreifen, i, i	to understand; seize
ein-fallen,†[1] ie, a, ä	to occur (*to one's mind*)
in den Sinn kommen,† a, o	to come to one's mind
die Seele, -, n	soul

156

der Gedanke, ns, n	thought
denken, a, a (an *a.***)**	to think (of)
nach-denken (über *a.***)**	to meditate (on), reflect
das Gedächtnis, ses, se	memory, remembrance
(sich) erinnern [an *a.***]**	to remind [of] (to remember)
die Übereinkunft, -, ¨e	agreement
überein-kommen,† a, o	to agree
die Entscheidung, -, en	decision, determination
das Andenken, s, -	remembrance, keepsake
die Erinnerung, -, en	remembrance, recollection

157

die Einbildungskraft	power of imagination
(un)würdig	(un)worthy
die Vernunft, -, *n.p.*	reason, judgment
vernünftig	reasonable, judicious
diskutieren	to discuss, debate
überzeugen	to convince
behaupten	to affirm, maintain
die Meinung, -, en	opinion, intention
meinen	to think, say, mean
bejahen	to answer in affirmative

[1] **es fiel mir ein,** it occurred to me.

158

verneinen	to deny, answer in negative
die Sicherheit, -, en	certainty
(un)sicher	sure, (un)safe (insecure)
(un)gewiß	sure, true, (un)certain
sich irren	to make a mistake
der Irrtum, (e)s, ¨er	error
wagen	to dare, risk
der Zweifel, s, -	doubt
zweifeln	to doubt
weifelhaft	doubtful, dubious

9

weifeln (an *d.*)	to despair (of)
erzweiflung, -, en	despair, desperation
der Argwohn, (e)s, *n.p.*	suspicion
verdächtig	suspicious, suspected
(ver)trauen (*dat.*)	to trust
vertrauen (auf *a.*)	to trust (in, to)
das Vertrauen, s, *n.p.*	trust, confidence
vertrauenswürdig	trustworthy
mißtrauisch	distrustful, suspicious
das Mißtrauen, s, *n.p.*	distrust

160

der Wunsch, (e)s, ¨e	wish
wünschen	to wish
das Geheimnis, ses, se	secret
bewilligen	to grant, consent to
der Wille, ns, *n.p.*	will, determination
die Willenskraft, -, ¨e	will power
wollen	to be willing, will, wish
(frei)willig	willing (voluntary)
beschließen, o, o	to decide (to, on)
(un)entschlossen	(un)determined, (un)decided

161

zögern	to hesitate
die Fähigkeit, -, en	ability, capability
(un)fähig	(un)able, (in)capable
die Begabung, -, en	talent, (natural) gift
der Charakter, s, e	character, temper
die Laune, -, n	humour (*good or bad*); whim
das Gefühl, (e)s, e	sensation, sentiment
die Freude, -, n	joy, pleasure, delight
die Fröhlichkeit, -, en	gaiety, mirth
froh	glad

162

heiter	clear, gay, serene
munter	lively
traurig	sad
die Traurigkeit, -, en	sadness, melancholy
(sich) betrüben	to grieve
der Kummer, s, *n.p.*	grief, sorrow
sich bekümmern (um)	to fret, be distressed *or* anxious
der Genuß, (ss)es, ¨(ss)e	enjoyment, pleasure
genießen, o, o	to enjoy (*the use of*); *also* eat *or* drink
(un)zufrieden	(dis)pleased, (dis)contented

163

die Zufriedenheit, -, en	contentment
gefallen,[1] ie, a, ä (*dat.*)	to please
die Gefälligkeit, -, en	kindness, favour
gefällig	obliging
mißfallen,[2] ie, a, ä (*dat.*)	to displease
die Mühe, -, n	pain, trouble
der Seufzer, s, -	sigh
seufzen	to sigh
sich beklagen (über *a.*)	to complain (of)
die Klage, -, n	complaint, grievance

[1] Also impers.: es gefällt ihm nicht in dieser Stadt.
[2] Impers.: es mißfällt mir, I dislike it.

164

weinen	to weep
die Träne, -, n	tear
niedergeschlagen	depressed, downcast
die Hoffnung, -, en	hope
hoffen	to hope
warten (auf *a.*)	to wait (for)
erwarten	to wait for, expect
die Erwartung, -, en	expectation
die Geduld, -, *n.p.*	patience
(un)geduldig	(im)patient

165

der Trost, (e)s, *n.p.*	comfort, consolation
trostlos	inconsolable
trösten	to comfort
der Mut, (e)s, *n.p.*	spirit, courage
mutig	courageous
ermutigen	to encourage
entmutigen	to dishearten
der Griff, (e)s, e	grip, grasp; handle
(er)greifen,[1] i, i	to seize
besänftigen	to soften, calm

166

die Sanftmut, -, *n.p.*	gentleness, meekness
ruhelos	restless, disquieted
besorgt (um)	anxious, concerned (for)
sorgenfrei	free from care
die Furcht, -, *n.p.*	fright, fear
fürchten	to fear
sich fürchten (vor *d.*)	to be afraid (of)
furchtbar	terrible, fearful
furchtsam	timid
Angst,[2] *f.* -, ¨e (haben)	fear, anxiety (to be afraid)

[1] See also group 227.
[2] Used as adj.: **Mir ist angst (vor),** I am afraid (of); **mir wird angst,** I am getting uneasy.

167

(er)schrecken	to frighten
erchrecken,† a, o, i	to be frightened, terrified
schrecklich	terrible, awful
zittern (vor *d.*)	to tremble, shake (with)
das Staunen, s, *n.p.*	astonishment, surprise
(er)staunen[1] (über *a.*)	to be astonished, surprised (at)
das Wunder, s, -	wonder, miracle, marvel
sich (ver)wundern (über *a.*)	to wonder, be surprised (at)
wunderbar	wonderful, amazing
die Verwunderung, -, *n.p.*	surprise, astonishment

168

die Überraschung, -, en	surprise
das Gewissen, s, -	conscience
gewissenhaft	conscientious, scrupulous
der Gewissensbiß, (ss)es, (ss)e	remorse
die Reue, -, *n.p.*	repentance
reuig	penitent
bereuen	to repent of, be sorry for
es reut mich	I repent
die Zustimmung, -, en	assent
zu-stimmen	to assent, agree to

169

die Gnade, -, *n.p.*	favour, grace
die Barmherzigkeit, -, en	mercy
die Wohltätigkeit	benevolence
die Wohltat, -, en	benefit, kindness
das Mitleid, (e)s, *n.p.*	pity, sympathy
die Leidenschaft, -, en	passion
(un)sympathisch	(un)congenial
die Gunst, -, *n.p.*	favour, goodwill
begünstigen	to favour
(un)günstig (*dat.*)	(un)favourable

[1] **erstaunen (*not* staunen)** can also be used transitively; **ich habe ihn erstaunt,** I surprised him.

170

die Freundschaft, -, en	friendship
(un)freundlich	(un)friendly, (un)kind
der Freund, (e)s, e	friend
liebenswürdig	amiable, lovable
die Liebenswürdigkeit, -, en	amiability
nett	nice, pretty, pleasant
der Haß, (ss)es, *n.p.*	hatred
hassen	to hate
widerwärtig	odious, hateful
die Verachtung, -, *n.p.*	contempt, scorn

171

verachten	to despise, scorn
verächtlich	contemptible, despicable
(sich) erzürnen	to irritate (get angry)
zornig (auf *a.*)	wrathful, angry (at, with)
der Zorn, (e)s, *n.p.*	wrath, anger, rage
der Streit, (e)s, e	quarrel, dispute
streiten, i, i	to fight
(sich) ärgern (über *a.*)	to vex, offend (be vexed at)
(sich) versöhnen	to reconcile (be reconciled)
(un)versöhnlich	forgiving, conciliatory (irreconcilable)

172

die Vorsicht, -, *n.p.*	prudence, (pre)caution
die Nachsicht, -, *n.p.*	indulgence
die Absicht, -, en	aim, intention
(un)beständig	steady, (in)constant (variable)
die Eigenschaft, -, en	quality
der Vorzug,[1] (e)s, ¨e	preference, advantage, priority
die Tugend, -, en	virtue
tugendhaft	virtuous
das Laster, s, -	vice
lasterhaft	vicious

[1] **Er hat den Vorzug vor, he is preferred to, he has the advantage over.**

173

ergeben (*dat.*)	devoted, addicted to
sich ergeben,[1] **a, e, i**	to become addicted to
der Mangel, s, ¨- (**an** *d.*)	want, absence, lack (of)
mangeln[2] (**an** *d.*), *imp.*	to be wanting (in)
Mangel leiden, i, i (**an** *d.*)	to be in want (of)
die Sitte, -, n	custom, use; morals
(un)sittlich	(im)moral
die Sittlichkeit, -, *n.p.*	morality
die Gewohnheit, -, en	habit, custom
gewöhnlich	usual, ordinary, general

174

	[(to)
sich gewöhnen (**an** *a.*)	to be used, accustomed
prahlen (**mit**)	to boast (about), show off
die Güte, -, *n.p.*	goodness, kindness
gütig	kind
die Schlechtigkeit, -, en	badness, wickedness
die Dankbarkeit	gratitude, gratefulness
(un)dankbar	(un)grateful
(ver)danken (*dat.*)	to thank (to owe)
die Ehrlichkeit	honesty
die (Un)Ehre, -, n	(dis)honour

175

(un)ehrlich	(dis)honest, (dis)honour-
ehrwürdig	venerable [able
(ent)ehren	to (dis)honour
die Bescheidenheit	modesty
bescheiden	modest, discreet
(un)verschämt	bashful, abashed (shame-
die Schande, -, n	shame; disgrace [less)
schändlich	shameful
sich schämen (**wegen**)	to be ashamed (of)
die Kühnheit, -, en	boldness

1 See also group 228.
2 **mir mangelt Zeit** *or* **es mangelt mir an Zeit.**

176

(toll)kühn	daring (foolhardy)
schüchtern	shy, timid, bashful
die Schüchternheit, -, *n.p.*	shyness, bashfulness
(all)gemein	common (general)
die Höflichkeit, -, en	politeness
(un)höflich	(im)polite
grüßen	to greet, salute
der Gruß, es, ¨e	salutation, greeting
der Abschied, (e)s, e	farewell, departure
der Neid, es, *n.p.*	envy

177

neidisch	envious
beneiden	to envy
die Sparsamkeit	thrift, economy
sparsam	economical
(er)sparen	to save, economize
der Verschwender, s, -	spendthrift
freigebig	generous
die Freigebigkeit	generosity
die Selbstsucht, -, *n.p.*	selfishness
selbstsüchtig	selfish

178

der Egoist, en, en	egoist
der Geiz, es, *n.p.*	avarice, greed
geizig	avaricious, mean
der Geizhals, es, ¨e	miser
die Wahrheit, -, en	truth
wahrscheinlich	likely, probable
wahr	true
falsch	false, wrong
lügen	to lie, tell a lie
die Lüge, -, n	lie, falsehood

179

der Lügner, s, -	liar
der Heuchler, s, -	hypocrite
offenherzig	frank, open-hearted
der Freimut, (e)s, *n.p.*	frankness
die Genauigkeit	accuracy, exactness
die Pünktlichkeit	punctuality
die (Un)Treue, -, *n.p.*	(un)faithfulness
(un)treu	(un)faithful
feig(e)	timid, cowardly
die Feigheit	cowardice

180

der Feigling, s, e	coward
die Wut, -, *n.p.*	rage, fury
wütend	raging, furious
die Beleidigung, -, en	offence, insult
beleidigen	to offend, insult
die Entschuldigung, -, en	excuse, apology
entschuldigen	to excuse
die Schuld, - (en)	guilt, fault (*pl.* debts)
die Bosheit, -, en	malice, wickedness
böse	bad, wicked

181

böse (auf einen über etwas)	angry (with someone about something)
bösartig	malicious, malignant
artig	well-behaved, good
demütig	humble
die Demut, -, *n.p.*	humbleness, humility
der Hochmut, (e)s, *n.p.*	haughtiness, pride
der Stolz, es, *n.p.*	pride, arrogance
stolz (auf *a.*)	proud, haughty (about)
eitel	vain, conceited
die Eitelkeit	vanity, conceit

182

frech	impudent, insolent
hartnäckig	stubborn, obstinate
die Hartnäckigkeit	stubbornness
(un)mäßig	(im)moderate, (in)temperate
nüchtern	sober
die Nüchternheit	sobriety, soberness, moderation
die (Be)trunkenheit	drunkenness
betrunken	drunk
der Trinker, s, -	drinker, drunkard
das Verbrechen, s, -	crime, offence

183

der Verbrecher, s, -	criminal, convict
der Mörder, s, -	murderer
(er)morden	to murder
der (Selbst)Mord, (e)s, e	murder (suicide)
der Räuber, s, -	robber, thief
der Dieb, (e)s, e	thief
der Raub, (e)s, *n.p.*	robbery, plunder
der Diebstahl, s, ¨e	theft, larceny, robbery
stehlen, a, o, ie	to steal
rauben	to rob, steal, plunder

184

das Vergehen, s, -	misdemeanour, legal offence
sich vergehen, i, a	to commit an offence; sin
begehen, i, a, *tr.*	to commit (*error, crime*); *also* celebrate
der Verräter, s, -	traitor
der Verrat, (e)s, *n.p.*	treason
verraten, ie, a, ä	to betray
verführen	to seduce
die Rache, -, *n.p.*	revenge, vengeance
(sich) rächen (an *d.*)	to revenge (oneself) on
rachsüchtig	revengeful, vindictive

DIE GESELLSCHAFT—SOCIETY

185

das Vaterland, (e)s, ¨er	native country
die Heimat, -, en	home, native land
der Eingeborene, n, n	native (*of primitive countries*)
die (Land)Straße, -, n	street, road (highway)
die Hauptstraße, -, n	main street
die Gasse, -, n	lane, alley, back street
die Allee, -, n	avenue, boulevard
der Fußgänger, s, -	passer-by, pedestrian
der Bürgersteig, (e)s, e	pavement
der Verkehr,[1] s, *n.p.*	traffic

186

der Kreisverkehr	roundabout (*traffic*)
das Plakat, (e)s, e	placard, poster
an-schlagen, u, a, ä	to post up, stick (*bills*)
der Weg, (e)s, e	way, road
der Pfad, (e)s, e	path
der (Last)Wagen, s, -	carriage, car (wagon, lorry)
der Kutscher, s, -	coachman, cabman
die Kutsche, -, n	carriage, cab
die Straßenbahn, -, en	tram(way)
der Straßenbahnwagen, s, -	tramcar

187

die Untergrundbahn	underground railway
das Pflaster, s, *n.p.*	paved surface (*of streets, etc.*)
der Platz, es, ¨e	square
der Park, (e)s, s	park, public garden
überschreiten, i, i (*tr.*)	to cross *or* step over
der Straßenübergang	pedestrian crossing
das (Stadt)Viertel	town, ward, district, quarter
der Bezirk, (e)s, e	district, borough
die Umgebung, -, en	surroundings, environs
umgeben, a, e, i	to surround

[1] See also group 394.

188

die Vorstadt, -, ¨e	suburb
der Sekretär, s, e	secretary
die Privatsekretärin	lady private secretary
die (Polizei)Behörde, -, n	(police) authority
der Polizist, en, en	policeman
der Schutzmann, s, ¨er	policeman
das (Geschäfts)Lokal, s, e	premises
die Niederlage, -, n	warehouse; *also* defeat
der Laden, s, ¨-	shop
der Ladentisch, (e)s, e	counter

189

der Wirt,[1] es, e (-in)	landlord (landlady)
das Wirtshaus, es, ¨er	inn
der Gastwirt, (e)s, e	innkeeper, hotelkeeper
ein-kehren† (bei)	to put up, be staying (at)
der Gasthof, es, ¨e	hotel
das Hotel, s, s	hotel
die Pension, -, en	board; boarding-house
das Restaurant, s, s	restaurant
die Verpflegung, -, en	board and attendance
die Unterkunft, -, ¨e	lodgings

190

Kost und Wohnung	board and lodgings
die Regierung, -, en	government
regieren	to rule, reign
nach-folgen† (*dat.*)	to follow, succeed
die Politik, -, *n.p.*	politics; policy
der Politiker, s, -	politician
der Herrscher, s, -	ruler, sovereign
die Monarchie, -, n	monarchy
der Kaiser, s, - (-in)	emperor (empress)
der König, s, e (-in)	king (queen)

[1] Cf. group 343.

191

kaiserlich	imperial
die Krone, -, n	crown
krönen	to crown
der Tron, (e)s, e	throne
der Prinz, en, en	prince (*son of ruler*)
die Prinzessin, -, nen	princess
der Fürst, en, en (-in)	prince (princess)
der Titel, s, -	title
der Untertan, s, en	subject (*of a country*)
die Obrigkeit,[1] -, *n.p.*	authorities, *pl.* (*of State*)

192

die Volksangehörigkeit	nationality
das Reich, (e)s, e	realm, kingdom, empire
die deutsche Bundesrepublik	the German Federal Republic
der Republikaner, s, -	republican
der (Bundes)Präsident, en, en	president (of the German Federal Republic)
der Vorsitzende, n, n	chairman
die Gesandtschaft, -, en	embassy
der Gesandte, n, n	ambassador
der Konsul, s, n	consul
das Konsulat, (e)s, e	consulate

193

der Staat, (e)s, en	state
der Rat, (e)s, ¨e	councillor; counsellor
der Rat,[2] (e)s	counsel, advice
(be)raten, ie, a, ä	to advise
der Verwalter, s, -	administrator
verwalten	to administer, manage
die Verwaltung, -, en	management, administration
der (Zu)Stand, (e)s, ¨e	state, position, situation
der Minister, s, -	secretary of state
der Ministerpräsident	Prime Minister

[1] Cf. die Behörde in group 188 for local authority or board.
[2] Plural Ratschläge.

194

der Ministerrat, (e)s, ¨e	Cabinet
der Bundeskanzler, s, -	the Federal Chancellor
der Außenminister	Minister of Foreign Affairs
der Innenminister	Home Secretary
der Finanzminister	Chancellor of the Exchequer
das Kriegsministerium, s, ien	War Office
das Kultusministerium[1]	Ministry of Education
der Bund, es, ¨e	federation, alliance; *also*
der Bundestag, (e)s	Federal Diet [band
der Bundesrat, (e)s	Federal Council

195

das Parlament, (e)s, e	parliament
der Abgeordnete, n, n	Member of Parliament
die Verfassung, -, en	constitution
die Sitzung, -, en	session, meeting, sitting
die Beratung, -, en	deliberation; counsel
(ver)schieben, o, o	to push, shove (postpone,
debattieren	to debate [put off)
(miß)billigen	to (dis)approve
an-nehmen, a, o, i	to adopt, accept
ab-lehnen	to decline, refuse

196

die Verordnung, -, en	ordinance, decree
verkünden	to proclaim
aus-führen	to execute, carry out
die Wahl, -, en	election; choice
das Wahlrecht, (e)s, e	suffrage, franchise
wählen	to choose, vote for, elect
die Stimme, -, n	vote; voice
einstimmig	unanimous
die Einigkeit, -, *n.p.*	unanimity, concord
(un)einig	(dis)united

[1] lit. Ministry of Education and Public Worship.

197

der Stadtrat, (e)s, ¨e	town council; town
das Rathaus, es, ¨er	town hall [councillor
der Bürgermeister, s, -	mayor, provost
der Bürger, s, - (-in)	citizen
die Bürgerschaft, -, *n.p.*	the citizens
die Arbeiterpartei, -, en	Labour Party
die Justiz, -, *n.p.*	justice (*administration*)
die Gerechtigkeit	justice, justness
das Recht, (e)s, e	right, law; duty
das Unrecht, (e)s, *n.p.*	wrong, injury

198

(un)gerecht	(un)just, (un)righteous
richtig	right, correct
der Richter, s, -	judge
der Gerichtshof, (e)s, ¨e	law court [justice
das Gericht, (e)s, e	judgment; court of
das Urteil, (e)s, e	judgment, sentence
die Verhandlung, -, en	proceedings, trial
das Gesetz, es, e	law
die Gesetzgebung, -, en	legislation
(un)gesetzlich	(il)legal

199

vermachen	to bequeath
der Erbe, n, n	heir, legatee
das Erbe, s, *n.p.*	legacy, inheritance
erben	to inherit
das Testament, (e)s, e	will
vor-laden, u, a, ä	to summon
der Prozeß, (ss)es, (ss)e	lawsuit, action
der Rechtsanwalt, (e)s, ¨e	lawyer, barrister
der Staatsanwalt, (e)s, ¨e	public prosecutor
der Klient, en, en	client

200

schwören, o, o	to swear (on oath), take [an oath
der Geschworene, n, n	juryman
der Schwur, (e)s, ¨e	oath
der Zeuge, n, n	witness
bezeugen	to bear witness to, certify
das Zeugnis, ses, se	testimony; certificate
die Überzeugung, -, en	conviction, belief [1]
auf frischer Tat ertappen	to catch in the act
der Beweis, es, e	evidence, proof
die Aussage, -, n	deposition, declaration

201

das Recht verletzen	to break the law
die Anklage, -, n	accusation
an-klagen (*gen.*)	to accuse (of)
verleumden	to slander, to defame
der Angeklagte, n, n	accused, defendant
gestehen, a, a	to confess, admit, own
sich (un)schuldig bekennen, a, a	to plead (not) guilty
für schuldig erklären	to convict
für unschuldig erklären	to pass verdict of not [guilty
die Verteidigung, -, en	defence

202

verteidigen	to defend
verbieten, o, o	to forbid, prohibit
die Begnadigung, -, en	pardon
die Lossprechung, -, en	acquittal
die Verurteilung, -, en	sentence, condemnation
verurteilen	to condemn, sentence
Berufung ein-legen (gegen *a.*)	to appeal (against)
die Todesstrafe, -, n	death penalty
das Gefängnis, ses, se	prison, jail
das Zuchthaus, es, ¨er	convict prison

[1] To the best of my belief, **nach meiner besten Überzeugung.**

203

ein-kerkern	to imprison
der Gefangene, n, n	prisoner
fangen, i, a, ä	to catch, seize
verhaften	to arrest
der Henker, s, -	hangman, executioner
hin-richten	to execute
die christliche Religion, -, en	Christian religion
religiös	religious
fromm	pious, devout
der Schöpfer, s, -	Creator; *also* founder

204

(er)schöpfen	to draw [*water, etc.*] (exhaust)
(er)schaffen,[1] u, a	to create
Gott, es, ¨er (¨-in)	God (goddess)
der Abgott, es, ¨er	idol
göttlich	divine
allmächtig	omnipotent, almighty
der Erlöser, s, -	Redeemer
der Heiland, s, *n.p.*	Saviour
erlösen	to redeem; deliver
der Heide, n, n	heathen

205

heidnisch	pagan
verhindern	to prevent, hinder
die zehn Gebote	the Ten Commandments
gebieten, o, o	to command
das Christentum, (e)s, *n.p.*	Christianity
der Christ, en, en (-in)	Christian
Christus, i[2]	Christ
die Bibel, -, n	Bible
der Protestant, en, en (-in)	Protestant
protestantisch	protestant

[1] Cf. **schaffen** in group 242. [2] Declined as in Latin: **nach Christo, nach Christi Geburt; Jesus Christus** is either invariable or declined.

206

der Katholik, en, en (-in)	(Roman) Catholic
katholisch	catholic
der Jude, n, n (¨-in)	Jew (Jewess)
jüdisch	jewish
beichten	to confess, go to confession
bekehren (zu)	to convert (to)
der Ketzer, s, -	heretic
die Ketzerei, -, en	heresy
der (Un)Gläubige, n, n	(un)believer
glauben (an *d.*)	to believe (in)

207

der (Aber)Glaube, ns, *n.p.*	faith, belief (superstition)
die Kirche, -, n	church
der Dom, (e)s, e	cathedral
die Kapelle, -, n	chapel; *also* orchestra
der Kaplan, (e)s, ¨e	chaplain
der Altar, (e)s, ¨e	altar
die Messe, -, n	mass
der Segen, s, -	blessing, benediction
segnen	to bless
(ver)fluchen[1]	to curse

208

der Geistliche, n, n	clergyman
die Gemeinde, -, n	congregation; parish
predigen	to preach
die Predigt, -, en	sermon
das Evangelium, s, ien	gospel
der heilige Geist, (e)s	Holy Ghost
heilig	holy, sacred, saint[2]
der Apostel, s, -	Apostle
der Jünger, s, -	disciple
der Himmel, s, -	heaven, sky

[1] **fluchen means also to swear, blaspheme, use bad language.**

[2] **Cf. Sankt Peter, Sankt Anton, etc. (der heilige Peter, der heilige Antonius). Die Epistel St Pauli an die Römer** (Luther), **der Brief des heiligen Apostels Paulus an die Römer** (Cath.).

209

himmlisch	heavenly, celestial
der (Erz)Engel, s, -	(arch)angel
selig	blessed, happy; *also* deceased[1]
geweiht	consecrated
weihen	to consecrate
der Teufel, s, -	devil
teuflisch	devilish, diabolical
die Hölle, -, n	hell
der Gottesdienst, es, e	divine service
das Opfer, s, -	offering, sacrifice; victim

210

das Vaterunser, s, -	Lord's Prayer
das Gebet, (e)s, e	prayer
beten	to pray
die Inbrunst, -, *n.p.*	fervour, ardour
die Sünde, -, n	sin
sündigen	to sin
der Sünder, s, -	sinner
taufen	to baptize, christen
die Taufe, -, n	baptism, christening
der Papst, es, ¨e	pope

211

der (Erz)Bischof, (e)s, ¨e	(arch)bishop
der Priester, s, -	priest
der Pfarrer, s, -	parson, priest
der Pastor, s, en	(*protestant*) clergyman
der Abt, (e)s, ¨e	abbot
die Äbtissin, -, nen	abbess
die Abtei, -, en	abbey
das Kloster, s, ¨-	convent, monastery
der Mönch, (e)s, e	monk
die Nonne, -, n	nun

[1] In such phrases as: **mein seliger** *or* **verstorbener Bruder,** my deceased brother; **mein Vater selig,** my late father.

212

der Pilger, s, - (-in)	pilgrim
das Fest, es, e	feast, festival, fête
die Feier, -, n	celebration, festival
feiern	to celebrate; *also* rest from one's work
feierlich	solemn
der Silvesterabend, s, *n.p.*	New Year's Eve
das Neujahr, s, *n.p.*	New Year
das Geschenk, (e)s, e	present, gift
schenken	to give, make a present of
fasten	to fast

213

die Fastnacht, -, *n.p.*	Shrove Tuesday
der Karfreitag, (e)s, e	Good Friday
(die) Ostern, *pl.*	Easter
die Auferstehung	resurrection
(die) Pfingsten, *pl.*	Whitsuntide
(die) Weihnachten, *pl.*	Christmas
das Heer, (e)s, e	army
exerzieren	to drill
der Exerzierplatz, es, ¨e	drill-ground, esplanade
die Fahne, -, n	flag, banner

214

die Wehrpflicht, -, en	military service
die Zucht, -, *n.p.*	discipline
der Rekrut, en, en	recruit, conscript
rekrutieren	to enlist
der Soldat, en, en	soldier
die Truppe, -, n	troops, *pl.*
der Offizier, s, e	officer
der Unteroffizier, s, e	N.C.O.
der Feldwebel, s, -	sergeant-major
der Rang,[1] (e)s, ¨e	rank; *also* class[1]

[1] **ersten Ranges, first class, first rate. See also group 370.**

215

der (Ober)Befehlshaber, s, -	commander(-in-chief)
der Feldmarschall, s, ¨e	field-marshal
der Oberst, en, en	colonel
der General, s, ¨e	general
der Hauptmann,[1] s	captain
der (Ober)Leutnant, s, s	2nd lieutenant (1st —)
der Befehl, (e)s, e	command
befehlen	to order, command
befehligen	to command (*army*)
der Orden, s, -	order (*religious or military*)

216

ordentlich	tidy, regular, ordinary
außerordentlich	extraordinary
sonderbar	odd, strange, singular
die (Un)Ordnung, -, en	(dis)order, arrangement
die Infanterie, -, n	infantry
die Kavallerie, -, n	cavalry
der Artillerist, en, en	artillery-man
die Kanone, -, n	(*big*) gun, cannon
das Geschütz, es, e	(*big*) gun
die (Hand)Granate, -, n	shell (hand grenade)

217

explodieren† (*intr.*)	to explode
platzen† (*intr.*)	to burst, explode
das Pulver, s, *n.p.*	gunpowder
die Munition, -, en	ammunition
die Bombe, -, n	bomb, shell
bombardieren	to shell, bombard
die Beschießung, -, en	bombardment
beschießen, o, o	to fire at, on; bombard
erschießen, o, o	to shoot dead
sprengen	to blow up; *also* sprinkle, water

[1] Plural Hauptleute.

218

der Pionier, s, e	pioneer, sapper
der Sanitäter, s, -	medical orderly
die Wache, -, n	watch, guard
Posten stehen	to mount guard
Wache ab-lösen	to change guard
die Garnison, -, en	garrison
die Kaserne, -, n	barracks
das Regiment, (e)s, er	regiment
die Abteilung, -, en	detachment, section
(ab-)teilen	to divide, share (divide up)

219

die Verstärkung, -, en	reinforcement
die Ausrüstung, -, en	equipment
aus-rüsten	to arm, equip
der Tornister, s, -	knapsack
die Uniform, -, en	uniform
der Helm, (e)s, e	helmet
die (Feuer)Waffe, -, n	(fire)arm, weapon
ab-feuern	to fire, discharge
(ent)waffnen	to (dis)arm
das (Maschinen)Gewehr, (e)s, e	(machine) gun, rifle

220

die Pistole, -, n	pistol
(ent)laden, u, a, ä	to (un)load
die Kugel, -, n	bullet
das Geschoß, (ss)es, (ss)e	projectile, bullet
die Patrone, -, n	cartridge
das Schwert, (e)s, er	sword
der Säbel, s, -	(*broad*) sword
das Bajonett, (e)s, e	bayonet
der Dolch, (e)s, e	poniard, dagger
erdolchen	to stab to death

221

die Marine, -, n	navy
der Seemann,[1] s	sailor, seaman
die Flotte, -, n	fleet, navy
das Geschwader, s, -	squadron
der Steuermann, s, ¨er	navigator, mate
steuern	to steer, pilot
das Steuer, s, -	helm, rudder
das Schiff, (e)s, e	vessel, boat, ship
die Schiffahrt, -, *n.p.*	navigation
sich ein-schiffen	to embark

222

das (Ruder)Boot, (e)s, e	(rowing) boat
das Kriegsschiff, (e)s, e	warship, man-of-war
der Kreuzer, s, -	cruiser
der Dampfer, s, -	steamer
der Dampf, (e)s, *n.p.*	steam
an Bord	on board
(aus-)laden, u, a, ä	to (un)load; *also* summon
das Ausladen, s, *n.p.*	unloading
die Ladung, -, en	cargo, load
das Unterseeboot, (e)s, e	submarine, U-boat

223

schleppen	to tow, haul, drag, trail
der Schlepper,[2] s, -	tug, tow-boat
die Überfahrt, -, en	passage, crossing
die Seereise, -, n	voyage
der Passagier, s, e	passenger
die Kabine, -, n	berth, cabin
das (Ver)Deck, s, s	deck
der Mast, (e)s, en	mast
das Segel, s, -	sail
segeln‡	to sail

[1] Plural Seeleute. [2] See also group 344.

224

das Seil, (e)s, e	rope, cordage
das Tau, (e)s, e	cable, rope
die Mannschaft,[1] -, en	crew; *also* team
(den) Anker werfen, a, o, i	to cast anchor
sinken,† a, u	to sink (*intr.*)
(ver)senken	to sink (*tr.*)
das Wrack, (e)s, e	wreck
Schiffbruch (er)leiden,[2] i, i	to be shipwrecked
das Signal, s, e	signal, call
ein Zeichen (s, -) machen	to make a sign

225

der Leuchtturm, s, ¨e	lighthouse
der Hafen, s, ¨-	port, harbour
der Kai, s, s	quay, wharf
die Werft, -, en	dockyard, wharf
(den) Krieg erklären	to declare war
Krieg führen (mit)	to wage war (upon)
kriegerisch	warlike
der Krieger, s, -	warrior
der Feind, (e)s, e	enemy
feindlich	hostile, inimical

226

der (General)Stab, s, ¨e	(general) staff
der Feldzug, s, ¨e	campaign
ins Feld ziehen,† o, o	to take the field
die Belagerung, -, en	siege
belagern	to besiege
befestigen	to strengthen; *also* fasten
die Festung, -, en	fortress
die Besetzung, -, en	occupation
der Wall, es, ¨e	rampart, embankment
der Graben, s, ¨-	trench, ditch

[1] See also groups 381 and 382.

[2] Or **schiffbrüchig werden** *or* **sein**

227

der Schützengraben, s, ¨-	trench, entrenchment
(aus-)graben, u, a, ä	to dig (dig out, excavate)
aus-kundschaften	to reconnoitre
der Spion, (e)s, e	spy
spionieren (*intr.*)	to spy
der Angriff, (e)s, e	attack
(an-)greifen, i, i	to seize, grasp (to attack)
verteidigen	to defend
der Sturm, es, ¨e	assault, storm
stürmen	to storm, assault

228

die Erstürmung, -, en	the taking by storm
der Ausfall, (e)s, ¨e	sally, sortie
der Hinterhalt, (e)s, e	ambush
übergeben, a, e, i (*tr.*)	to surrender, hand over
sich ergeben,[1] **a, e, i**	to surrender (*intr.*)
die Einnahme, -, n	taking, capture
das (Zusammen)Treffen	engagement (encounter)
treffen, a, o, i	to hit; meet with
das Gefecht, (e)s, e	fight
fechten, o, o, i	to fight; *also* fence

229

eine Schlacht liefern	to give battle
der Kampf, (e)s, ¨e	fight, strife
kämpfen	to fight, struggle
tapfer	gallant, courageous
die Schanze, -, n	entrenchment, fortification
zurück-schlagen, u, a, ä	to repulse
der Rückzug, (e)s, ¨e	retreat
sich zurück-ziehen, o, o	to retreat
plündern	to plunder
die Gefangenschaft, -, en	captivity

[1] See also group 173.

230

die Flucht, -, en	flight, escape
fliehen,† o, o	to flee
entkommen,† a, o	to escape
verfolgen	to pursue; persecute
die Verfolgung, -, en	pursuit; persecution
entscheiden, ie, ie	to decide
der Sieg, (e)s, e	victory, triumph
(be)siegen	to win, conquer (defeat)
siegreich	victorious, triumphant
der Sieger, s, -	victor

231

der Besiegte, n, n	the conquered
unbesiegbar	invincible
der Waffenstillstand, s, ¨e	armistice
der Friede, ns, *n.p.*	peace
der (Friedens)Vertrag, (e)s, ¨e	(peace) treaty
Frieden schließen, o, o	to make peace
Bedingungen stellen	to make one's conditions
das Lager auf-schlagen, u, a, ä	to pitch the camp
das Lager auf-heben, o, o	to break up the camp
das Zelt, (e)s, e	tent

232

das Manöver, s, -	manœuvres
das Lazarett, (e)s, e	ambulance, military hospital
der Verwundete, n, n	wounded man
der Invalide, n, n	disabled man
der Held, en, en (-in)	hero (heroine)
die Heldentat, -, en	exploit
die Auszeichnung, -, en	distinction, decoration
die Verzierung, -, en	decoration (*ornament*)
das eiserne Kreuz, es, e	Iron Cross
der Friedhof, (e)s, ¨e	cemetery

DIE GESELLIGE TÄTIGKEIT— SOCIAL ACTIVITY

233

der Pächter, s, -	farmer, tenant
das (Pacht)Gut, (e)s, ¨er	estate, property (farm[1])
der Gutsherr, n, en	landlord, landowner
der Hof, (e)s, ¨e	yard, court
der Hühnerhof	poultry yard
der (Spring)Brunnen, s, -	well, spring (fountain)
der Kuhstall, (e)s, ¨e	cowhouse
der Pferdestall	(horse) stable
die Scheune, -, n	barn
das Stroh, (e)s, *n.p.*	straw

234

das Futter, s, *n.p.*	food, fodder
füttern	to feed, fodder
das Heu, (e)s, *n.p.*	hay
der Heuboden, s, ¨-	hayloft
der Karren, s, -	cart
der Fuhrmann, s, ¨er	carter
der Schubkarren, s, -	wheelbarrow
das Geschirr,[2] (e)s, e	harness; *also* utensils, implements
an-spannen (aus- —)	to put to (take out)
das Gespann, (e)s, e	team (*of horses*), yoke

235

das Leder, s, -	leather
der Sattel, s, ¨-	saddle
der Sattler, s, -	saddler
der Zügel, s, -	rein, bridle
die Peitsche, -, n	whip
ziehen,[3]† o, o	to pull, draw, march, move on
stoßen, ie, o, ö	to push
der Ackerbau, s, *n.p.*	agriculture
der Ackersmann, s, ¨er	ploughman
der Landwirt, (e)s, e	farmer (*proprietor*)

[1] **Pachtgut,** *lit.* leasehold estate, from **pachten,** to rent or take on lease.
[2] See also group 68.
[3] Takes **sein** only when *intr.*, i.e. with the meaning of motion.

236

landwirtschaftlich	agricultural
der Acker, s, ¨-	field, acre
das Feld, es, er	field
die Wiese, -, n	meadow
das Gras, es, ¨er	grass
der Bauer, n, n (-in)	farmer, peasant
rüstig	active, vigorous
betreiben, ie, ie (*tr.*)	to carry on, work at
pflügen	to plough
der Pflug, (e)s, ¨e	plough

237

der Dünger, s, *n.p.*	dung, manure
der Mist, (e)s, *n.p.*	dung, manure
säen	to sow
die Saat, -, en	seed; sowing
zerstreuen	to scatter
mähen	to mow, reap
die Mähmaschine, -, n	reaping-machine
die Sense, -, n	scythe
die Sichel, -, n	sickle
die Ernte, -, n	harvest, crop

238

ernten	to reap, gather
die Harke, -, n	rake
die Hacke, -, n	hoe
die Spitzhacke, -, n	pickaxe
die Axt, -, ¨e	axe
der Spaten, s, -	spade
das Loch, (e)s, ¨er	hole
hohl	hollow
höhlen	to hollow out, excavate
das Korn, (e)s, ¨er	corn, grain

239

dreschen, o, o, i	to thresh
die Dreschmaschine, -, n	threshing-machine
das Getreide, s, -	corn, grain, cereals
der Weizen, s, *n.p.*	wheat
die Ähre, -, n	ear (*of corn*)
die Garbe, -, n	sheaf
der Hafer, s, *n.p.*	oats
die Gerste, -, *n.p.*	barley
der Roggen, s, *n.p.*	rye
der Klee, s, *n.p.*	clover

240

der Haufen, s, -	heap
auf-häufen	to heap up, accumulate
häufig	frequent
selten	rare, scarce; seldom
seltsam	strange
der Handel, s, *n.p.*	commerce, trade
handeln	to trade
das Handelshaus, es, ¨er	commercial house
die Filiale, -, n	branch
aus-führen (ein-—)	to export (import)

241

die Einfuhr, -, *n.p.*	import trade
die Ausfuhr, -, *n.p.*	export trade
der Verein, (e)s, e	association, union
(sich) vereinigen	to unite (together)
der Gefährte, n, n (-tin)	companion
der Geselle, n, n	journeyman; *also* fellow
sich zu-gesellen (*dat.*)	to associate with
sich verbinden mit	to associate with
der Verband, (e)s, ¨e	union; *also* bandage
die Gewerkschaft, -, en	trade union

242

der Händler, s, -	dealer, shopkeeper
der Kaufmann, s, -leute	tradesman, merchant
der Käufer, s, -	buyer, purchaser
kaufen	to buy, purchase
das Geschäft, (e)s, e	business; *also* shop
geschäftig	busy, active
schaffen,[1] **u, a**	to do, make, create
die Geschäftsverbindung, - en	business connection
die Rechnung, -, en	bill, account
ein Konto eröffnen (bei)	to open an account (with)

243

in Betracht ziehen, o, o	to take into account *or* consideration
in Rechnung mit	in account current with
Konto übertragen, u, a, ä auf (*d.*)	to place to the credit of
Soll und Haben	debit and credit
vernichten	to cancel, annihilate
null und nichtig	null and void
auf Credit	on credit
in Raten	by instalments
bares Geld, (e)s, er	ready money
das Kleingeld, (e)s, er	small change

244

bar bezahlen	to pay cash
gegen Barzahlung	for cash
das Depositum, s, -ten	deposit
deponieren	to deposit
die Ware, -, n	goods, merchandise
das Warenhaus, es, ¨er	department store, stores
besucht	well patronized *or* frequented
das Muster, s, -	pattern, sample
die Sache, -, n	thing, object; affair
das Ding, (e)s, e	thing

[1] Also regular.

245

billig	cheap
teuer	dear, expensive
die Verpackung, -, en	packing
(aus-)packen	to pack (unpack)
ein-packen	to pack up
das Gepäck, (e)s, *n.p.*	luggage
ein-wickeln (aus-—)	to wrap up (unwrap)
(sich) vor-bereiten	to prepare (oneself)
bereit (für *or* **zu)**	ready (for *or* to)
(fort-)schicken	to dispatch, send (off)

246

der Transport, (e)s, e	carriage, conveyance
transportieren	to transport
die Fracht, -, en	freight; railway charges
das Porto, s, *n.p.*	postage
portofrei	post free *or* carriage paid
frei ins Haus	delivered free of charge
die Lieferung, -, en	delivery (*of goods*)
die Eilbestellung, -, en	special delivery
das Büro, s, s	office (*place of business*)
das Kontor, s, e	office (*counting house*)

247

der Geschäftsführer (-in)	manager(ess)
der Chef, s, s	chief, head
vor-stehen, a, a (*dat.*)	to manage, administer
der Vorsteher, s, - (-in)	manager, director
der Buchhalter, s, - (-in)	bookkeeper, accountant
das Amt, (e)s, ¨er	office, function
der (ein) Beamte(r)	official, functionary
(ohne) Beschäftigung	(out of) employment *or* occupation
(sich) beschäftigen	to give employment to (occupy oneself)
(un)beschäftigt	busy, (un)occupied, (un)employed

248

an-stellen	to employ
die Schreibmaschine, -, n	typewriter
der Stenotypist, -, en (-in)	shorthand typist
der Stenograph, en, en	shorthand writer
die Stenographie, -, n	shorthand
stenographieren	to take down in shorthand
ein guter Kauf, (e)s, ¨e	a great bargain
Einkäufe machen	to make purchases
zum Verkauf	for sale
(im Kleinen) verkaufen	to sell (retail)

249

stückweise	retail
en Gros	wholesale
der Ausverkauf, (e)s, ¨e	clearance sale
die Versteigerung, -, en	auction sale
versteigern	to sell by auction
der Kunde, n, n (-in)	customer
der Katalog, (e)s, e	catalogue
die Preisliste, -, n	price list
um jeden Preis	at all costs, at any price
geringer Preis, es, e	low price

250

fester Preis	fixed price
im Preise steigen,† ie, ie	to go up in price
fordern[1]	to demand, ask
der Betrag, es, ¨e	amount
die Kosten, *pl.*	cost, expense
der Kostenanschlag, s, ¨e	estimate
kostenfrei	gratuitous, free
kostbar	costly, expensive
im voraus	beforehand, in advance
die (Be)Zahlung, -, en	payment

[1] **Wieviel fordern Sie dafür?** How much do you want for it?

251

auf Abschlag	in part payment
der Kassierer, s, -	cashier
das Saldo, s, s	balance of an account
der Abschluß, (ss)es, ¨(ss)e	making up the accounts; statement; conclusion
die Schlußbilanz, -, en	balance sheet
übereinstimmend	all correct
die (Brutto)Einnahme	(gross) receipts
ein-nehmen, a, o, i	to receive; cash
die Ausgabe, -, n	expense; *also* edition
aus-geben, a, e, i	to spend; issue; distribute

252

empfangen, i, a, ä	to receive
den Empfang bescheinigen	to acknowledge receipt
der Gewinn, (e)s, e	profit
der Verlust, (e)s, e	loss
die Anleihe, -, n	loan
leihen, ie, ie	to borrow, lend
der Wucher, s, *n.p.*	usury
der Wucherer, s, -	usurer
der Gläubiger, s, -	creditor
der Schuldner, s, -	debtor

253

in Schulden geraten, ie, a, ä	to run into debt
schuldig sein[1]	to owe, be indebted; *also* guilty
der Bankrott, (e)s, e	bankruptcy
Bankrott machen	to become bankrupt
die Bank, -, en	bank
der Bankier, s, s	banker
die Banknote, -, n	banknote
die (Spar)Kasse, -, n	cash-box, pay-desk; till (savings bank)
die Ersparnisse,[2] ***pl.***	savings
Zahlungen ein-stellen	to stop payments

[1] Er ist mir 10 Mark schuldig, he owes me 10 marks. See also group 201.
[2] Cf. group 177.

254

das Kapital, s, ien	capital
die Zinsen,[1] *pl.*	interest
die Rente, -, n	rent, annuity
die Börse, -, n	Exchange; *also* purse
die Aktie, -, n	share
der Aktieninhaber, s, -	shareholder
wechseln	to change, exchange
aus-tauschen (*tr.*)	to exchange, change
gelten, a, o, i	to be worth; *also* be valid
der Wert (e)s, e	value, worth

255

schätzen	to value; *also* esteem
der Diskont, s, e	discount, deduction
der Rabatt (e)s, e	discount, rebate
ab-ziehen, o, o (von)	to deduct (from)
der (Verrechnungs)Scheck, (e)s, e[2]	(crossed) cheque
auf Sicht zahlbar	payable at sight
an den Vorzeiger zahlbar	payable to bearer
an die Order zahlbar	payable to order
die Unterschrift, -, en	signature
unterschreiben, ie, ie	to sign

256

die Überschrift, -, en	heading
einen Wechsel ziehen, o, o, auf (*a.*)	to draw (bill) on
zur Verfallzeit[3]	at *or* on maturity (*of a bill*)
fällig sein	to fall due
verfallen,† ie, a, ä	to decay; *also* become due
verfallen	now due
datiert	dated
zur rechten Zeit	in due course
rechtzeitig	in (good) time, punctually
ohne weitere Benachrichtigung	without further notice

[1] The sing. **der Zins, es,** is seldom used, except in compounds **zinsfrei, Zinsrechnung.** [2] Plural also **Schecks.** [3] Or **bei Verfall.**

257

die Münzstätte	Mint
die Münze, -, n	money, coin
die Geldmünze	coin, piece of money
gültig	current, valid
eine (Reichs)Mark[1]	1 mark
50 Pfennig(e)	½ mark
das Fünfmarkstück, (e)s, e	5-mark piece
der Franken,[2] **s, -**	franc
der Schilling, s, e	shilling
das Pfund Sterling	£ sterling

258

der Reichtum, s, ¨er	wealth, riches
reich	rich, wealthy
der Reiche, n, n	rich man
(sich) bereichern	to enrich (grow rich)
erwerben, a, o, i	to acquire, earn, gain
das Eigentum, s, ¨er	property
eigen	own
das Vermögen, s, -	fortune; *also* power, ability
vermögend	wealthy, opulent
der Wohlstand, (e)s, ***n.p.***	prosperity, comfort

259

wohlhabend	well-to-do
das Einkommen, s, -	income
die Einkünfte, ***pl.***	revenues, income
die Armut, -, ***n.p.***	poverty
arm	poor
die Dürftigkeit, -, ***n.p.***	poverty, need
bedürftig	needy
elend	miserable, wretched
ins Elend geraten, ie, a, ä	to come to poverty
um ein Almosen bitten, a, e	to ask for alms

[1] No plural, e.g. 2 Mark, 2 marks. [2] Also der Frank, s, en.

260

betteln	to beg, ask charity
der Bettler, s, - (-in)	beggar
unterstützen	to support, aid
im Notfall	in case of necessity, if need be
bei-stehen, a, a (*dat.*)	to stand by, assist
spenden	to give (*charity*); contribute
das Gewicht, (e)s, e	weight
gewichtig	heavy, weighty
wiegen, o, o	to weigh (*tr. and intr.*)
die Waage, -, n	scales, weighing-machine

261

(ver)messen, a, e, i	to measure (survey)
das Maß, es, e	measure
der Zoll, (e)s; 3 Zoll breit	inch; 3″ wide
der Fuß, es; 5 Fuß hoch	foot; 5′ high
die Unze, -, n	ounce
das metrische System, s, e	metric system
der Quadratmeter,[1] s, -	= 1·2 sq.yd. (5 sq.m. = 6 sq. yd.)
der Kilometer, s, -	= 1000 m. ($\frac{5}{8}$ mile)
das Ar, s, e	= 100 sq.m. (40$\frac{1}{2}$a. = 1 acre)
das Hektar, s, e	= 100 a. (1 ha. = 2$\frac{1}{2}$ acres)

262

das Gramm, (e)s, e	(28·3 g. = 1 oz.; 1 lb. = 454 g.)
das Kilo(gramm)	= 1000 g. (5 kg. = 11 lb.)
das Pfund, (e)s, e	= $\frac{1}{2}$ kg. (1$\frac{1}{4}$ lb.)
der Zentner, s, -	= 50 kg. (1 cwt.)
die Tonne, -, n	= 1000 kg. (20 cwt.)
der Liter, s, -	= 1$\frac{3}{4}$ pt. (4$\frac{1}{2}$ l. = 1 gal.)
der Deziliter, s, -	= $\frac{1}{10}$ l. (a wineglassful)
die Industrie, -, n	industries, manufactures
das Gewerbe, s, -	business, trade, profession
die Gewerbeschule, -, n	technical school

[1] Meter = 3ft. 3in.; yard = 91 cm. (Meter, Liter also neuter.)
N.B. All equivalents are only approximate, for comparison purposes.

263

gedeihen,† ie, ie	to thrive, prosper, increase
der Fabrikant, en, en	maker, manufacturer
die Fabrik, -, en	factory, works
die Manufaktur, -, en	manufacture, works
die Schutzmarke, -, n	trademark
die Gasanstalt, -, en	gasworks
die Glasfabrik, -, en	glass works
die Tuchfabrik, -, en	cloth mill
maschinell hergestellt[1]	machine made
der Maschinist, en, en	mechanical engineer; engine-man

264

der Ingenieur, s, e	civil engineer
das Handwerk, s, e	handicraft, trade
das Werkzeug, (e)s, e	instrument, tool
die Schraube, -, n	screw
der Schraubenzieber, s, -	screwdriver
die Spinnerei, -, en	spinning-mill
die Weberei, -, en	weaving; weaving-mill
der Weber, s, - (-in)	weaver
das Gewebe, s, -	texture, fabric; tissue
der Lohn, (e)s, ¨e	reward, compensation, wages

265

der Meister, s, - (-in)	master (mistress)
der Lehrling, s, e	apprentice
die Lehrzeit, -, en	apprenticeship
der Sachverständige, n, n	expert, specialist
die Sachkunde, -, ***n.p.***	expert knowledge
(un)gewandt	smart, clever (clumsy, awkward)
(un)geschickt	fit, skilful (unskilled, clumsy)
(un)tüchtig	able, (in)capable, (un)qualified
(un)erfahren	(in)experienced
(un)fähig	(in)capable, (un)fit

[1] Also **maschinell gefertigt** and **maschinenhergestellt.**

266

das Erzeugnis, ses, se	product, production
erzeugen	to produce
müßig	idle, lazy
der Müßiggang, (e)s, *n.p.*	idleness
die Einstellung, -, en	cessation, stoppage
die Streikenden, *pl.*	men on strike, strikers
Arbeit ein-stellen	to cease work, (go on) strike
der Zimmermann, s, -leute	carpenter
der Tischler, s, -	joiner, cabinetmaker
der Möbelschreiner, s, -	cabinetmaker

267

die Einrichtung, -, en	arrangement, furnishing
der Leim, (e)s, *n.p.*	glue
leimen	to glue
(an-)kleben	to stick, *intr.* (stick, *tr.*, [*or* paste)
kleb(e)rig	sticky, adhesive
der Hammer, s, ¨ -	hammer
(ver)nageln	to nail (nail up)
die Säge, -, n	saw
sägen	to saw
der Uhrmacher, s, -	clockmaker

268

der Papierhändler, s, -	stationer
der Fischhändler, s, -	fishmonger
der Kurzwarenhändler	haberdasher
der Lebensmittelhändler	provision-dealer, grocer
der Handwerker, s, -	artisan
der Müller, s, -	miller
die (Wind)Mühle, -, n	(wind)mill
mahlen	to grind
das Mehl, es, e	meal, flour
der Fleischer, s, -	butcher (*North Germ.*)

269

der Metzger, s, - butcher (*South Germ.*)
die Fleischerei *or* Metzgerei, -, en butcher's [shop
der Friseur, s, e hairdresser
sich das Haar schneiden lassen, ie, a, ä to get one's hair cut
sich rasieren to shave (oneself)
der Rasierapparat, (e)s, e safety razor
die Klinge, -, n blade
das Parfüm, s, e perfume, scent
parfümiert scented, perfumed
der Tabakshändler, s, - tobacconist

270

der Zigarrenladen, s, ¨ - tobacconist's shop
der Tabak, s, e tobacco
die (Filter)Zigarette, -, n (tipped) cigarette
eine Pfeife stopfen to fill a pipe
die Röhre, -, n tube, pipe (*not smoking*)
die Reise, -, n journey, travel
reisen‡ (nach) to travel, go (to)
der (Geschäfts)Reisende, n, n (commercial) travel- [ler
der Tourist, en, en tourist
die Tour, -, en tour, excursion

271

die Eisenbahn, -, en railway
der Bahnhof, s, ¨ e station
der Bahnsteig, (e)s, e platform
die Schiene, -, n rail
das Geleise, s, - track, rails
entgleisen† to run off the rails
zusammen-stoßen,† ie, o, ö to collide
die Katastrophe, -, n catastrophe
der Fahrplan, s, ¨ e time-table
der Personenzug, (e)s, ¨ e passenger train

272

der Schnellzug, (e)s, ¨e	express *or* fast train
der D-Zug, (e)s, ¨e	through train
der Güterzug, (e)s, ¨e	goods train
an-kommen,† a, o	to arrive
die Ankunft, -, ¨e	arrival
ab-fahren,† u, a, ä	to leave, start, depart
die Abfahrt, -, en	departure
der Bahnhofsvorsteher, s, -	station master
der Wartesaal, (e)s, -säle	waiting room
die (Rück)Fahrkarte, -, n	(return) ticket

273

hin und zurück	there and back
zurück-kehren†	to return
die Rückkehr, -, *n.p.*	return
der Schalter, s, -	booking-office; counter [(*post office*)
die Sperre,[1] -, n	(platform) barrier
nach-sehen, a, e, ie	to examine
reklamieren	to demand back; put in [a claim
die Lokomotive, -, n	engine
der Zugführer, s, -	driver
der Heizer, s, -	stoker

274

der Schaffner, s, -	guard; *also* bus conductor
der Abteil, (e)s, e	compartment
das (Gepäck)Netz, es, e	(luggage) rack
der Wagen erster Klasse	first-class carriage
der Schlafwagen, s, -	sleeping-car
der Speisewagen, s, -	dining-car
der Gepäckwagen, s, -	luggage van
der Gepäckträger, s, -	porter
der Gepäckschein, (e)s, e	luggage ticket
der (Hand)Koffer, s, -	trunk (suitcase)

[1] Cf. sperren and compounds in groups 309 and 395.

275

auf-geben, a, e, i	to register (*luggage*); *also* [to give up
die Station, -, en	stop, station
die (Bus)Haltestelle, -, n	stopping-place (bus stop)
der Aufenthalt, (e)s, e	stop; stay, sojourn
sich auf-halten, ie, a, ä	to stay, stop, reside
ein-steigen,† ie, ie	to get into (*train, bus*)
aus-steigen,† ie, ie	to alight, get out *or* off
auf- und ab-steigen†	to step up and down
der Zoll, (e)s, ¨e	customs, duty
das Zollamt, (e)s, ¨er	customs house

276

verzollen[1]	to pay duty on
zollpflichtig	dutiable, liable to duty
zollfrei	free from duty
die Zollgrenze, -, n	customs frontier
der (ein) Zollbeamte(r)	customs officer
untersuchen	to search, examine
die Untersuchung, -, en	examination
die Steuer, -, n	tax, duty
der Paß, (ss)es, ¨(ss)e	passport
der Ausweis, es, e	document

277

der Personalausweis	identity paper
sich aus-weisen, ie, ie	to prove one's identity
das Postamt, (e)s, ¨er	post office
der Postbeamte, n, n	post office clerk *or* officer
postlagernd	poste restante
auf der Post auf-geben, a, e, i	to post (*a letter*)
der Brief, (e)s, e	letter
der Briefwechsel, s, -	correspondence
das Briefpapier, s, e	writing- *or* note-paper
mit-teilen	to communicate, inform

[1] **Haben Sie etwas zu verzollen?, Have you anything to declare? Waren verzollen, to clear goods at the customs house.**

278

die Mitteilung, -, en	communication, notice
umgehend[1]	by return of post; immediate
postwendend	by return of post
die Postkarte, -, n	postcard
die Ansichtskarte, -, n	picture postcard
der Briefträger, s, -	postman
die Brieftasche, -, n	pocket-book
der Karton, s, s	pasteboard
die Pappe	card- *or* pasteboard
der Briefkasten, s, -	letter-box, pillar-box

279

die Leerung,[2] **-, en**	collection (*of letters*)
aus-tragen, u, a, ä	to deliver (*letters*)
die Postbestellung,[3] **-, en**	delivery of letters
der Umschlag, (e)s, ¨e	envelope
die Adresse, -, n	address
die Frankierung, -, en	prepaid postage
frankiert	prepaid, postpaid
eine (Brief)Marke auf-kleben	to affix a stamp
(ver)siegeln	to seal
das Siegel, s, -	seal

280

der Stempel, s, -	stamp, postmark
stempeln	to mark, stamp
Drucksache, -, n	printed matter
(als) Postpaket	(by) parcel post
das Paket, (e)s, e	parcel
ein-schreiben, ie, ie (lassen)	to register
der Einschreibebrief, (e)s, e	registered letter
die Einschreibegebühr, -, en	registration fee
die Postanweisung, -, en	postal *or* money order
(ab-)senden,[4] **a, a**	to send (send away, dispatch)

[1] **Mit umgehender Post** *or* **umgehend antworten,** reply by return; **umgehende Antwort dringend erbeten,** an answer by return is urgently requested. [2] Cf. **leeren in group 68.**
[3] See also group 246. [4] **Also regular.**

281

der Absender, s, -	sender
der Empfänger, s, -	receiver, recipient
die Zusendung, -, en	sending, dispatch
der Tarif, (e)s, e	tariff
das Telegraphenamt, (e)s, ¨er	telegraph office
die drahtlose Telegraphie	wireless telegraphy
der Draht, (e)s, ¨e	wire
telegraphieren	to telegraph, wire
das Telegramm, (e)s, e	telegram
der Fernschreiber, s, -	teleprinter

282

das Brieftelegramm	letter telegram, night—
der Eilbrief	express letter
(die) Luftpost	by air (airmail)
die Depesche, -, n	dispatch, telegram
das Telephon, (e)s, e	telephone
der Fernsprecher, s, -	telephone
an-rufen, ie, u	to ring up; *also* implore
melden	to announce
die Meldung, -, en	announcement, report
der (Eil)Bote, n, n	(special) messenger

DAS WELTALL—THE UNIVERSE

283

die Natur	nature
die Schöpfung, -, en	creation
die Welt, -, en	world
das Himmelsgewölbe	firmament
die Wolke, -, n	cloud
umwölkt, wolkenlos	cloudy, cloudless
der Stern, (e)s, e	star
das Gestirn, (e)s, e	stars,[1] *pl.*
die Sternwarte, -, n	observatory
der Planet, en, en	planet

[1] But also any heavenly body, *e.g.* the moon.

284

glänzend	bright, sparkling, glittering
der Mond, (e)s, e	moon
die (Sonnen)Finsternis, -, se	darkness (eclipse of the sun)
finster	dark; gloomy
verdunkeln	to darken, obscure
die Sonne, -, n	sun
der Strahl, (e)s, en	ray, beam
der Mondschein, (e)s, *n.p.*	moonlight
(er†)scheinen,[1] ie, ie	to shine; seem, look (appear)
die Morgenröte, -, n	dawn

285

die Abendröte, -, n	twilight, dusk
der Sonnenaufgang, (e)s, ¨e	sunrise
der Sonnenuntergang	sunset
auf-gehen,† i, a	to rise (*of the sun*)
unter-gehen,† i, a	to set (*of the sun*)
die Erde, -, *n.p.*	earth
das Erdbeben, s, -	earthquake
die Wüste, -, n	desert
öde	desert, waste
das Tal, (e)s, ¨er	valley

286

die Ebene, -, n	plain
eben	level, flat
der Hügel, s, -	hill
der Abhang, (e)s, ¨e	slope (*of hill*)
der Berg, (e)s, e	mountain
das Gebirge, s, -	mountain range
die Gebirgskette, -, n	chain of mountains
das Vorgebirge	cape, promontory
sich erstrecken	to extend
der Gipfel, s, -	top, summit (*of mountain*)

[1] **erscheinen lassen,** to bring out, to publish; **soeben erschienen** (*of books*), just published, just out.

287

der Gletscher, s, -	glacier
die Lawine, -, n	avalanche
der Felsen, s, -	rock
felsig	rocky, like a rock
steil	steep, precipitous
schroff	rugged, steep
der Abgrund, (e)s, ¨e	abyss, precipice
die Küste, -, n	coast
der Strand, (e)s, *n.p.*	shore, strand, beach
die Klippe, -, n	cliff, rock

288

die See, -, *n.p.*	sea
der See, s, n	lake
die Flut, -, en	flood, high tide
die Ebbe, -, n	ebb *or* low tide
die Welle, -, n	wave
die Woge, -, n	billow, wave
der Schaum, (e)s, ¨e	foam; *also* froth
die Meerenge, -, n	straits
die (Halb)Insel, -, n	island (peninsula)
die Quelle, -, n	spring, source

289

	[*(of a river)*
entspringen,† a, u (aus)	to spring out of; rise on
der Wasserfall, s, ¨e	waterfall
der Bach, (e)s, ¨e	brook, stream, rivulet
der Fluß, (ss)es, ¨(ss)e	river, stream[1]
flüssig	fluid, liquid
(über-)fließen,† o, o	to flow, run (overflow)
der Strom, (e)s, ¨e	(large) river
tief	deep
die Tiefe, -, n	depth
die Brücke, -, n	bridge

[1] Cf. upstream, up the river, **fluß-** *or* **stromaufwärts**; downstream, down the river, **fluß-** *or* **stromabwärts.**

290

das Ufer, s, -	bank (*of a river*)
die Überschwemmung, -, en	flood
der Damm, (e)s, ¨e	dam, dike
die Mündung, -, en	mouth (*of a river*)
der Teich, (e)s, e	pond
der Sumpf, (e)s, ¨e	marsh, bog
das Wetter, s, -	weather
die Witterung, -, en	weather, wind, etc.
gemäßigt	temperate, moderate
mild	mild; *also* soft, kind

291

kühl	cool
das Klima, s, s[1]	climate
währen	to last, continue
(sich) verändern	to change
veränderlich	changeable, unsettled
(un)beständig	(un)steady, (in)constant
das Baro-, Thermometer, s, -	barometer, thermometer
der Grad, (e)s, e	degree
die Luft, -, ¨e	air, breeze
der Luftzug, (e)s, ¨e	draught

292

der Wind, (e)s, e	wind
windig	windy
windstill	calm
wehen (*intr.*)	to blow
brausen	to rush, roar
das Gewitter, s, -	thunderstorm
der Sturm, (e)s, ¨e	storm, tempest
heftig	violent, intense
rasend	wild, mad, in a rage
heran-ziehen,† o, o	to approach, be coming

[1] Plural also Klimate.

293

vorüber sein	to be over *or* past
feucht	moist, humid, damp
die Feuchtigkeit, -, en	moisture, dampness
naß	wet
naßkalt	damp and cold
trocken	dry; arid, barren
ausgetrocknet	dried up, drained; *also* withered
die Dürre, -, n	aridity, dryness, drought
der Regen, s, -	rain
regnen; es regnet	to rain; it is raining

294

regnerisch	rainy
der Regenbogen, s, ¨-	rainbow
der (Regen)Schirm, (e)s, e	umbrella
der Sonnenschirm, (e)s, e	sunshade
der Tau, (e)s, *n.p.*	dew
es taut	dew is falling; *also* it is thawing
das Tauwetter, s, -	thaw
der Tropfen, s, -	drop
der Regenguß, (ss)es, ¨(ss)e	shower
der Blitz, es, e	lightning

295

der Donner, s, -	thunder
donnern; es donnert	to thunder; it is thundering
der Nebel, s, -	mist, fog
neb(e)lig	foggy, misty
der Schnee, s, *n.p.*	snow
schneien	to snow
der Hagel, s, *n.p.*	hail
das Eis, es, *n.p.*	ice
der Frost, (e)s, ¨e	frost
gefrieren,†[1] o, o, *imp.*	to freeze, be freezing

[1] Cf. **ich friere** and **mich friert**, both these forms taking **haben** as their auxiliary.

DIE TIERE — ANIMALS

296

das Haustier, (e)s, e	domestic animal
fressen, a, e, i	to eat (*of animals*)
saufen, o, o, äu	to drink (*of animals*)
der (Hof)Hund, (e)s, e	(watch)dog
an-binden, a, u	to chain, fasten
los-binden, a, u	to let loose, unfasten
bellen	to bark
beißen, i, i	to bite
heulen	to howl
wachsam	watchful

297

hüten	to guard, watch
das Maul, (e)s, ¨er	mouth (*of animals*)
der Schwanz, (e)s, ¨e	tail
die Pfote, -, n	paw
die Tatze, -, n	paw
die Katze,[1] -, n	cat
das Pferd, (e)s, e	horse
die Stute, -, n	mare
das Füllen, s, -	colt, foal
traben‡	to trot

298

galoppieren‡	to gallop
der Esel, s, -	ass, donkey
der Maulesel, s, -	mule
das Vieh, (e)s, *n.p.*	cattle
das Rind, (e)s, er	(horned) cattle
schlachten	to slaughter, kill
das Horn, (e)s, ¨er	horn
die Herde, -, n	herd, flock
weiden	to pasture *tr. and intr.*, graze
die Kuh, -, ¨e	cow

[1] Cf. der Kater, s, -, tom-cat.

299

melken,[1] o, o, i	to milk
der Ochs, en, en	ox
der Stier, (e)s, e	bull
das Kalb, (e)s, ¨er	calf
das Lamm, (e)s, ¨er	lamb
das Schaf, (e)s, e	sheep
der Schäfer, s, - (-in)	shepherd(ess)
der Hirt, en, en	herdsman, shepherd
die Ziege, -, en	goat
das (Wild)Schwein, (e)s, e	pig (wild-boar)

300

mästen (mit)	to fatten, feed (on)
das Kaninchen, s, -	rabbit
das Wild, (e)s, *n.p.*	game, venison
der Wilddieb, (e)s, e	poacher
wild	wild; savage
(ver)treiben, ie, ie	to drive (away)
lauern (auf *a.*)	to be on the watch (for)
zähmen	to tame, domesticate
zahm	tame, tractable, domesticated
blutdürstig	bloodthirsty

301

der Löwe, n, n, (-win)	lion(ess)
der Tiger, s, - (-in)	tiger (tigress)
zerreißen, i, i	to tear, rend
reißend	ferocious (*of beasts of prey*)
sich stürzen auf *a.*	to throw, rush, pounce upon s.o.
grausam	cruel
grimmig	grim, furious
der Wolf, (e)s, ¨e (¨-in)	wolf (she-wolf)
der Bär, en, en	bear
plump	clumsy; heavy-looking

[1] But also regular, except in the past part. **gemolken.**

302

der Elefant, en, en	elephant
das Kamel, (e)s, e	camel
der Hirsch, (e)s, e	stag, deer
die Hirschkuh, -, ¨e	hind
flink	quick, brisk, agile
rasch	quick, swift
das Reh, (e)s, e	roe, doe; deer
der Affe, n, n	monkey
der Fuchs, es, ¨e	fox
schlau	sly

303

der Hase, n, n	hare
die Ratte, -, n	rat
die Maus, -, ¨e	mouse
das Insekt, (e)s, en	insect [(harmless)
(un)schädlich	(not) injurious, noxious
der (Regen)Wurm, (e)s, ¨er	worm (earthworm)
die Seidenraupe, -, n	silkworm
die Raupe, -, n	caterpillar
sich krümmen	to twist oneself, cringe
krumm	crooked, bent

304

sich verwandeln	to change, transform
der Schmetterling, s, e	butterfly [oneself
die Mücke, -, n	gnat
saugen,[1] o, o	to suck
die Fliege, -, n	fly
der Flügel, s, -	wing
die Feder, -, n	feather, plume; *also* pen nib
das Gefieder, s,	feathers, *pl.* plumage
die Spinne, -, n	spider
das Spinn(en)gewebe, s, -	cobweb

[1] Also regular.

305

die Wespe, -, n	wasp
stechen, a, o, i	to sting, bite, prick
die Biene, -, n	bee
der Bienenkorb, s, ¨e	beehive
der Honig, s, *n.p.*	honey
das Wachs, es, *n.p.*	wax
die Ameise, -, n	ant
emsig	assiduous, active, diligent
die Heuschrecke, -, n	grasshopper
der Käfer, s, -	beetle

306

das Reptil, s, e[1]	reptile
die Schildkröte, -, n	tortoise, turtle
die Kröte, -, n	toad
der Frosch, es, ¨e	frog
die Schlange, -, n	serpent, snake
die Natter, -, n	adder, snake
kriechen,† o, o	to creep, crawl
der (Raub)Vogel, s, ¨-	bird (of prey)
raubgierig	rapacious
der Schnabel, s, ¨-	bill, beak

307

der Käfig, s, e	cage
der Spatz, en, en	sparrow
der Sperling, s, e	sparrow
zwitschern	to chirp, twitter
hüpfen	to hop; *also* skip
die Schwalbe, -, n	swallow
der Kanarienvogel, s, ¨-	canary
das Rotkehlchen, s, -	robin
der Fink, en, en	finch
der Gimpel, s, -	bullfinch

[1] Plural Reptilien when used generally, *e.g.* in a heading.

308

die Nachtigall, -, en	nightingale
die Lerche, -, n	lark
die Elster, -, n	magpie
der Rabe, n, n	raven
der Kuckuck, s, s	cuckoo
die Amsel, -, n	blackbird
der Storch, (e)s, ¨e	stork
die Eule, -, n	owl
scheu	shy
das Nest, (e)s, er	nest

309

nisten	to build a nest
das Ei, (e)s, er	egg
der Hahn, (e)s, ¨e	cock
krähen	to crow
das Huhn, (e)s, ¨er	fowl, hen (*in general*)
die Henne, -, n	(*domestic*) hen
das Küken, s, -	chicken
ein-sperren	to shut up, confine
die Taube, -, n	pigeon, dove
die Gans, -, ¨e	goose

310

der Schwan, (e)s, ¨e	swan
der Papagei, (e)s, en[1]	parrot
der Puter, s, -	turkey
der Pfau, (e)s, en[1]	peacock
der Adler, s, -	eagle
der Geier, s, -	vulture
der Strauß, es, e	ostrich
der Falke, n, n	falcon, hawk
die Ente, -, n	duck
der Fisch, es, e	fish

[1] Also *gen.* en, *pl.* e.

311

der Stockfisch, (e)s, e	(*dried*) codfish[1]
die Schuppe, -, n	scale
die Gräte, -, n	fish-bone
der Karpfen, s, -	carp
die Forelle, -, n	trout
der Aal, (e)s, e	eel
der Lachs, es, e	salmon
der Hering, s, e	herring
die Sardine, -, n	sardine
die Scholle, -, n	plaice

312

das Weichtier, (e)s, e	mollusc
das Krustentier, (e)s, e	crustacean
die Auster, -, n	oyster
die Krabbe, -, n	crab
der Krebs, es, e	(*freshwater*) lobster, crayfish
der Hummer, s, -	(*sea*) lobster
der Walfisch, (e)s, e	whale
der Haifisch, (e)s, e	shark
der Seehund, (e)s, e	seal
das Walroß, (ss)es, (ss)e	walrus

DIE PFLANZEN — PLANTS

313

pflanzen	to plant
die Wurzel, -, n	root
der Stengel, s, -	stalk, stem
die Rinde, -, n	bark; *also* crust
(ent)sprießen, o, o	to sprout, shoot forth (spring up)
das Laub, (e)s, *n.p.*	foliage
belaubt	leafy
dicht	dense
lichten	to clear, thin (*of forests*)
das Blatt, (e)s, ¨er	leaf; *also* (news)paper

[1] For cod, see group 414.

314

der Dorn, (e)s, en	thorn
dornig	thorny
die Knospe, -, n	bud
keimen	to sprout, bud, spring up
die Blüte, -, n	blossom, bloom
(ver)blühen	to bloom, flower (fade, wither)
blühend	blossoming, blooming
die Blume, -, n	flower
pflücken	to pick, pluck, gather
der Blumentopf, (e)s, ¨e	flower-pot

315

sich entfalten	to open, develop
ab-brechen, a, o, i	to break off, pluck off
der Strauß, es, ¨e	bunch of flowers
der Kranz, es, ¨e	wreath, garland
flechten, o, o, i	to twist, interweave; plait
der Garten, s, ¨-	garden
der Gärtner, s, -	gardener
begießen, o, o	to water
die Gießkanne, -, n	watering-can
verwelken†	to wither, fade

316

verdorren†	to dry up
welk	withered
frisch	fresh
das (Blumen)Beet, (e)s, e	flower- *or* garden-bed
das Veilchen, s, -	violet
die Rose, -, n	rose
der Rosenstock, (e)s, ¨e	rose bush
der Mohn, (e)s, e	poppy
der Duft, (e)s, ¨e	fragrance, scent
duften	to smell sweet

317

das Stiefmütterchen, s, -	pansy
die Schlüsselblume, -, n	cowslip, primrose
die Kornblume	cornflower
die Glockenblume	harebell, bluebell
die Goldblume	chrysanthemum
das Maiglöckchen, s, -	lily of the valley
das Gänseblümchen	(*small*) daisy
die Tulpe, -, n	tulip
die Lilie, -, n	lily
der Lorbeer, s, en	laurel

318

die Nelke, -, n	carnation
die Levkoje, -, n	stock, gillyflower
der Goldlack, (e)s, e	wallflower
das Vergißmeinnicht, s, e	forget-me-not
der Gemüsegarten, s, ¨-	kitchen garden
der Zaun, es, ¨e	hedge, fencing, railing
ein-zäunen	to enclose, fence in
die Hecke, -, n	hedge
die Mohrrübe, -, n	carrot
die Steckrübe	turnip

319

die rote Rübe	beetroot
die Kartoffel, -, n	potato
(zer)stampfen	to mash (*potatoes*), crush
reinigen[1]	to clean; purify
die Zwiebel, -, n	onion
das Radieschen, s, -	radish
der Spargel, s, -	asparagus
der (Gift)Pilz, es, e	mushroom (toadstool)
das Gift, (e)s, e	poison, venom
giftig	poisonous, venomous

[1] Cf. group 402.

320

eßbar	edible, eatable
die (Essig)Gurke, -, n	cucumber (gherkin)
die Tomate, -, n	tomato
die Erbse, -, n	pea
die Bohne, -, n	bean
der Kohl, (e)s, *n.p.*	cabbage
der Blumenkohl	cauliflower
der Rosenkohl	Brussels sprouts
die Petersilie, -, *n.p.*	parsley
der Porree, s, s	leek

321

der Obstgarten, s, ¨-	orchard
das Obst, (e)s, *n.p.*	fruit (*proper*)
die Frucht, -, ¨e	fruit[1]; *also* field produce
(un)fruchtbar	fruitful, fertile (sterile)
reifen	to ripen, mature
(un)reif	(un)ripe
überreif	over-ripe
frühreif	precocious
saftig	juicy
der Saft, (e)s, ¨e	juice, sap

322

schütteln	to shake
ab-schneiden, i, i	to cut *or* saw off; amputate
aus-schneiden, i, i	to cut off, out, away
beschneiden, i, i	to prune, clip, trim
die Birne, -, n	pear; *also* (*electric*) bulb
der Birnbaum, (e)s, ¨e	pear-tree
die Kirsche, -, n	cherry
der Kirschbaum, (e)s, ¨e	cherry-tree
der Apfel, s, ¨-	apple
die Pflaume, -, n	plum; prune

[1] Also fig., e.g. fruits of s.o.'s work, profit, etc.

323

der Pfirsich, (e)s, e	peach
die Aprikose, -, n	apricot
die Nuß, -, ¨(ss)e	nut, walnut
die Haselnuß	hazelnut
die Kastanie, -, n	chestnut
die Apfelsine, -, n	orange
die Zitrone, -, n	lemon
die Pampelmuse, -, n	grapefruit
die Olive, -, n	olive
die Dattel, -, n	date, date-tree

324

die Palme, -, n	palm; *also* palm-tree
die Banane, -, n	banana
das Zuckerrohr, (e)s, e	sugar cane
der Strauch, (e)s, ¨er[1]	shrub, bush
der Erdbeerstrauch	strawberry plant
die Himbeere, -, n	raspberry
die Stachelbeere	gooseberry
die Johannisbeere	currant
die Traube, -, n	grape
die Rosine, -, n	raisin

325

die Rebe, -, n	vine
der Weinstock, (e)s, ¨e	vine-stock
der Weinberg, (e)s, e	vineyard
die Weinlese, -, n	grape-gathering; vintage
(auf-)lesen, a, e, ie	to gather, glean, pick up
der Winzer, s, -	vine- *or* wine-grower
die Kelter, -, n	wine-press
keltern	to press (*fruit*)
der Wald, (e)s, ¨er	forest, wood
waldig	woody, wooded

[1] **Plural also Sträuche.**

326

das Gehölz,[1] es, e	wood, thicket
das Gewächs, es, e	growth, plant
der (Pflanzen)Wuchs, ses, *n.p.*	growth (vegetation)
der Stamm, (e)s, ¨e	trunk, stem
der Ast, (e)s, ¨e	bough
der Zweig, (e)s, e	branch, twig
der Wipfel,[2] s, -	top (*of a tree*)
das Moos, es, e	moss
das Heidekraut,[3] (e)s, *n.p.*	heath, heather
das Unkraut, (e)s, *n.p.*	weed(s)

327

der Efeu, s, *n.p.*	ivy
der Holzhauer, s, -	woodcutter
fällen	to cut down, fell
um-hauen, ie, au	to fell
ab-holzen	to clear of trees
die Eiche, -, n	oak
die Buche, -, n	beech
die Esche, -, n	ash
die Ulme, -, n	elm
die Pappel, -, n	poplar

328

schlank	slim, slender
die Linde, -, n	lime-tree, linden
die Birke, -, n	birch
die Weide, -, n	willow; *also* pasture
die Tanne, -, n	spruce, fir
die Fichte, -, n	pine, fir
die Kiefer, -, n	Scots fir *or* pine
das Ebenholz, es, *n.p.*	ebony
das Mahagoni	mahogany
das Rosenholz	rosewood

[1] From Holz, see group 48. [2] Cf. der Gipfel in group 286.
[3] But die Heide, heath (moor).

DIE MINERALIEN[1] — MINERALS

329

das Metall, (e)s, e — metal
das Bergwerk, (e)s, e — mine
der Bergmann, (e)s, -leute — miner
das Erz, es, e — ore; *also* bronze
die Schmiede, -, n — forge, smithy
der Schmied, (e)s, e — smith, blacksmith
schmieden — to forge
das Eisen, s, *n.p.* — iron
eisern — iron (*adj.*), of iron
das Hufeisen, s, - — horseshoe

330

der Rost, (e)s, *n.p.* — rust
rosten — to rust
rostfrei — stainless
der Stahl, (e)s, e *or* ¨e — steel
das Kupfer, s, *n.p.* — copper
kupfern — copper (*adj.*), of copper
das Messing, s, *n.p.* — brass
das Zinn, s, *n.p.* — tin
biegsam — supple, flexible, pliable
biegen, o, o — to bend

331

das (Weiß)Blech, (e)s, e — sheet metal (tinplate)
das Blei, (e)s, *n.p.* — lead
löten — to solder
der Bleigießer, s, - — lead smelter
gießen, o, o — cast, found; *also* pour
das Gußeisen, s, *n.p.* — cast iron
die Gußform, -, en — mould
formen — to form, mould
der Hochofen, s, ¨- — blast furnace
das Zink, (e)s, *n.p.* — zinc

[1] Plural also **Minerale**, see footnote, p. 103.

332

die Bronze, -, n	bronze
das Nickel, s, ***n.p.***	nickel
das Aluminium, s, ***n.p.***	aluminium
das Silber, s, ***n.p.***	silver
das Quecksilber	mercury
das Gold, es, ***n.p.***	gold
golden	gold (*adj.*), of gold
vergolden	to gild
das Platin, s, ***n.p.***	platinum
der Steinbruch, (e)s, ¨e	quarry

333

der Steinmetz, en, en	stone-cutter
der Meißel, s, -	chisel
die Feile, -, n	file
aus-beuten	to work (*a mine*), exploit
der Kieselstein, s, e	(flint) pebble
der Kies, es, e	gravel
der Kiesweg, (e)s, e	gravel path
steinig	stony
versteinert	petrified
zerschlagen, u, a, ä	to beat to pieces, break

334

der Granit, (e)s, e	granite
der Marmor, s, e	marble
polieren	to polish
glatt	smooth, even; slippery
(ab-)glätten	to smooth, polish
der Kalk, (e)s, e	lime
der Schwefel, s, ***n.p.***	sulphur
der Edelstein, (e)s, e	precious stone, gem
(un)echt	genuine (sham)
wertlos	worthless, valueless

335

das Juwel, (e)s, e(n)	jewel
der Juwelier, (e)s, e	jeweller
das Kleinod, (e)s, e[1]	precious thing, jewel
(ein-)fassen	to seize, take (set)
die Einfassung, -, en	setting
prachtvoll	splendid, magnificent
herrlich	splendid, magnificent
die (Uhr)Kette, -, n	(watch) chain
fesseln	to chain, fetter
die Perle, -, n	pearl; *also* bead

336

die Perlmutter, -, ***n.p.***	mother-of-pearl
der Diamant, en, en	diamond
der Rubin, (e)s, e	ruby
der Smaragd, (e)s, e	emerald
das Email,[2] **s,** ***n.p.***	enamel
schmelzen,†[3] **o, o, i**	to smelt, melt
der Saphir, (e)s, e	sapphire
der Achat, (e)s, e	agate
der Opal, (e)s, e	opal
der Topas, es, e	topaz

[1] Plural also **Kleinodien.**
[2] Note **Emaillewaren,** enamel goods.
[3] Also regular when transitive.

PART II

The words in this section are supplementary to Part I. The numbers in brackets indicate the appropriate group in Part I to which the words in Part II belong.

THE HUMAN BODY

337 [1, 19]

der Reiz, e charm, attention
anziehend attractive, alluring
an-ziehen[1] to attract
weh painful, sore, aching
ein weher Finger a sore finger
mir tut der Kopf weh my head aches
mir *or* **mich schmerzt der Kopf** my head aches
schmerzen to be painful, hurt, grieve
der Unfall, ¨e accident
der Zufall chance *or* accident

338 [19–22, 24]

fiebern to have a temperature
die Pille, Tablette pill, tabloid
das Beruhigungsmittel tranquillizer
Reisekrankheitstabletten travel sickness pills
die Mullbinde (gauze) bandage
das Heftpflaster sticking *or* adhesive plaster
der Krankenwagen ambulance
die Röntgenstrahlen *m.pl.* X-rays
röntgen to X-ray
Trauer an- *or* **ab-legen um** to go into *or* out of mourning for

[1] See also groups 72 and 235.

THE FAMILY

339 [26–7]

sich verlieben (in *a.*) to fall in love (with)
sich verheiraten to get married
verheiratet married
neuvermählt newly married
die Vermählten bride and bridegroom
trauen to marry (*i.e. perform the ceremony*)
die Trauung wedding ceremony
das Standesamt, ¨er registry office
die Ehe marriage (*state of matrimony*)
ehelich matrimonial; legitimate (*of children*)

340 [26–7]

die Mitgift dowry
die Ehescheidung divorce
sich scheiden lassen (von) to obtain a divorce (from)
der Trauschein, e marriage lines *or* certificate
ledig single, unmarried
der Gatte, n, n, (-tin) husband (wife)
der Junggeselle, n, n bachelor
der Witwer, die Witwe widower, widow
der, die Verlobte, n, n fiancé, fiancée
sich verloben to become engaged

341 [29]

beleben to enliven, animate, put life into
wieder-beleben to revive
der künstliche Wiederbelebungsversuch, e[1] artificial respiration
die Überlebenden survivors
überleben to survive, outlive
lebenslänglich lifelong, for life
auf Lebenszeit for life
die Lebensversicherungsgesellschaft life insurance company
die Lebensverhältnisse, *n.pl.* living conditions
seinen Lebensunterhalt verdienen to earn one's living

[1] *lit.* artificial attempt at resuscitation.

342 [29–31, 37]

lebend(ig)	alive (lively; *also* alive)
lebhaft; leblos	lively; lifeless, dull
das schöne Geschlecht, er	the fair sex
die Lebensart	manners, good breeding
vornehm	refined, distinguished, aristocratic
das menschliche Wesen	human being
human	humane, humanitarian
das Menschenalter	generation, average life-time
die menschliche Natur	human nature
die Verspätung	delay

THE HOUSE

343 [39]

die Hausfrau	housewife
der Haushaltsplan, ¨e	budget
die Wirtschaft[1]	economy, management
wirtschaftlich	economical, thrifty
die Wirtschaftlehre	economics
die Wirtschaft führen	to do the housekeeping
die Wirtschafterin	housekeeper
die Stütze	lady help (*lit.* prop, support)
das Heim, e	home, homsestead, hostel
das Altersheim	old folk's home

344 [39–42]

heimisch	homely
heimatlos	homeless
das Fertighaus, ¨er	prefabricated house
das Mietshaus *or* **Mehrfamilienhaus**	tenement
der Häuserblock, ¨e *or* **die Mietshäuser**	large block of flats or houses
das Hochhaus *or* **der Wolkenkratzer**	skyscraper
der (Trocken)Bagger	excavator
der Erdbagger	bulldozer
der Raupenschlepper	caterpillar tractor
der Zement- *or* **Betonmischer**	cement *or* concrete mixer

[1]Cf. Volkswirtschaft, political economy. See also groups 189, 235–6, 401

345 [45–9]

die Schwelle	threshhold
die Stufe	step
die Vorhalle	entrance hall
das Haus brennt	the house is on fire
in Flammen	in flames
löschen	to extinguish
das Löschgerät, e	fire extinguisher
die Feuerwehr	fire brigade
der Feuerwehrsman, ¨ner	fireman
der Schlauch, ¨e	hose; tube (*flexible*)

346 [49]

der Stecker	plug
der Schalter	switch
die Steckdose	wall socket
ein- *or* **aus-schalten**	to switch on *or* off
die (Leitungs)Schnur,[1] **¨e**	flex
der Strom versagte	the current failed
die Sicherung	fuse; *also* safety-catch
der Gleich- *or* **Wechselstrom, ¨e**	direct *or* alternating current
der Kurzschluß, ¨(ss)e	short circuit
die Birne	bulb, electric lamp

347 [49, 56]

der Elektrizitätszähler	electric meter
die Gasuhr	gas meter
die Taschenlampe	torch
der Ventilator, en *or* **Lüfter**	ventilator, air-hole
mit Elektrizität betrieben	electric(ally operated)
mit Gas versehen	supplied *or* provided with gas
den Tee ein-schenken	to pour out the tea
Tee *or* **Kaffee kochen**	to make tea *or* coffee
Kaffee mit Sahne *or* **Milchkaffee**	white coffee
die Kaffee(filtrier)maschine	percolator

[1] Cf. **Leitung** (group 83) and **Schnur** (group 77).

348 [57–61]

das Butterbrot, e	(slice of) bread and butter
Butterbrot mit Schinken	ham sandwich
für sechs Personen decken	to set the table for six
das Salz reichen	to pass the salt
sich betrinken, a, u	to get drunk
das Trinkgeld, er	tip, gratuity
das (Trink)Glas, ¨er	glass (tumbler)
der Becher	beaker, mug
das Zitronenwasser; Selters-	lemonade; soda-[water
der Apfelsinensaft, ¨e	orange squash

349 [61–2]

der Apfelwein, e	cider
der Champagner	champagne
der Sekt, e	a dry, sparkling wine
der Schnaps, ¨e	spirits (*e.g. whisky, brandy*)
nahrhaft	nourishing, nutritious
das Schweinefleisch	pork
gehacktes Fleisch	mince
rösten	to grill, roast, toast (*bread*)
die Brühe	broth
der Vorrat, ¨e	stock, store, reserve

350 [62–3]

die Büchse	tin, can
das Büchsenfleisch	tinned or canned meat
der Büchsenöffner	tin opener
hart- *or* weichgekochtes Ei	hard *or* soft-boiled egg
Rühreier	scrambled eggs
das Spiegelei, er	fried egg
Spiegeleier mit Speck	bacon and eggs
verlorene Eier	poached eggs
das Omelett, e	omelette
das Schmalz, e	dripping, lard

351 [64, 66–7]

begehrenswert *or* **-würdig**	desirable
begierig (nach)	eager (for)
das Kochbuch, ¨er	cookery book
zum Kochen bringen, a, a	to bring to the boil
die Milch kocht *or* **läuft über**	the milk boils over
schmecken (wie, nach)	to savour, taste (like, of)
der Gasherd, e	gas cooker
der Temperaturregler	thermostat
der Dampfdruckkocher *or* **Dampfer**	pressure [cooker
der Kühlschrank,[1] ¨e	refrigerator

352 [67–8]

der Durchlauferhitzer	water heater
durchlaufend	continuous
der Kartoffelbrei, das -mus	mashed potatoes
die Kartoffelflocken, *f.pl.*	potato crisps
die Pommes frites,[2] *pl.*	chips
die Schale	shell, peel, skin, pod, husk
(ab-)schalen	to peel, pare, skin
das Faß, ¨(ss)er	barrel, cask
fassen	to contain; seize, grasp; comprehend
vergießen, o, o	to spill

353 [68–9]

die Geschirrabwaschmaschine	dishwasher
das Abwaschtuch, ¨er	dish cloth
ab- *or* **auf-waschen, u, a, ä**	to wash up
die Spülküche	scullery
der Spülstein, e	sink
der Müll	refuse, rubbish, sweepings
der Mülleimer; -wagen	dustbin; dust cart
putzen	to clean, polish
die Putzfrau *or* **Rein(e)machefrau**	charwoman
der Lappen	rag, piece of cloth

[1] Cf. Eisschrank, ice-box.

[2] French, pron. *pom frit.*

354 [69–72]

scheuern	to scour, scrub
der Scheuerlappen	floor cloth
der Staubsauger	vacuum cleaner
die Waschmaschine	washing machine
die Wäsche auf-hängen	to hang up the washing
auf- *or* **aus-trocknen** *tr.*	to dry (up)
aus-trocknen† *intr.*	to dry (up)
ab-trocknen	to wipe dry (*dishes*)
das Bügeleisen; bügeln	iron; to iron
das Bügelbrett, er	ironing-board

355 [73–4]

die (Baum)Wolle	wool (cotton)
die Wollwaren *f.pl.*	woollens
wollig	woolly
die Watte	cotton wool
farbecht	fast, of fast colour
lichtecht	fadeless, fast to light
die Konfektion	ready-made clothes
das Schneiderkleid, er	tailor-made suit
nach Maß	made to measure, tailor-made
ab- *or* **auf-messen, a, e, i**	to measure (*material*)

356 [75–81]

der Absatz, ¨e	heel (*of shoe*)
(be)sohlen	to sole *or* re-sole
das Schuhband, ¨er	shoe lace
die Schuhkrem,[1] s	shoe polish
die (Gürtel)Schnalle	(belt) buckle
(ab-)schnallen	to (un)buckle
auf-putzen	to dress up
die Sicherheitsnadel	safety pin
die Schleife	bow; *also* slip-knot
der Schlips, e	neck-tie, cravat

[1] Also **der Krem, e**; cf. **Hautkrem**, face cream; **Zahnkrem**, toothpaste.

GENERAL EDUCATION

357 [83–4]

die Bildung education, culture; *also* formation
höhere Bildung higher education
der akademische Grad *or* **Titel** university degree
promovieren to graduate, take one's degree
der Doktor, en doctor (*of the university*)
der Ehrendoktor honorary doctor
die Doktorwürde doctorate
höhere Studien postgraduate studies
der Forschungsarbeiter postgraduate research [worker
der (ein) Graduierte(r) graduate

358 [86, 88, 89]

der Gebrauch, ¨e use, usage; *also* custom
gebräuchlich customary, in use
zu eigenem Gebrauch for personal use
die Bedürfnisse *f.pl.* needs
der Bedarf, e (an) need (of), requirement, requisite
etwas nötig haben to need something
das Nötige besorgen to do all that is necessary
zerstreuen to spread, scatter
sich zerstreuen to amuse oneself
lesbar legible; worth reading

359 [89, 91]

eine Vorlesung halten, ie, a, ä (über *a.***)** to give a [lecture on
Vorlesungen hören to attend lectures
der Vorleser (-in) lecturer, reader
aus-lesen, a, e, ie to finish reading; *also* select
die Lesehalle reading room
die Reifeprüfung *or* **das Abitur, e** leaving examin-[ation
das Reifezeugnis, se leaving certificate
eine Rede machen to make a speech
einem ins Wort fallen to interrupt a person
einen unterbrechen, a, o, i to interrupt someone

360 [104]

der Verlag, e	publishing house
der Verleger	publisher
vergriffen	out of print
das Penguinbuch, ¨er	paperback
ein gebundenes Exemplar	a bound copy
ein Buch über (*acc.*)	a book on
die Presse	the press, newspapers
die Pressekonferenz	press conference
der Zeitungshändler	newsagent
die Zeitungsstand, ¨e	newspaper kiosk

361 [104–6]

der Nachrichtenredakteur, e	news editor
der Leitartikel	leading article, leader
Was gibt es Neues?	What is the news?
das Handelsblatt, ¨er	trade journal
das Rundfunkblatt	radio times
das Witzblatt[1]	comic paper
die Modezeitung	fashion magazine
neuzeitlich	up to date, recent
der Kulturmensch, en	civilized man
die Naturvölker *or* **Primitiven**	primitive peoples

362 [106–7]

die Zivilisation *or* **Gesittung**	civilization; good [manners
(un)gesittet	civilized, good-mannered (uncivilized)
barbarisch	barbaric, barbarous
zivil	civil (*non-military*)
der Zivilist, en, en	civilian
das Zivilrecht	civil law
das Rassenproblem, e	racial problem
die Rassenschranke	colour bar
der (ein) Farbige(r)	coloured man
die Großmächte *f.pl.*	the great powers

[1] Cf. group 144.

363 [108, 110]

der Aufstieg, e — ascent; *also* rise
auf-steigen,†[1] ie, ie — to ascend, rise
der Aufstieg und Fall — decline and fall
der Ferne (Nahe) Osten — Far (Near) East
der Mittelosten — Middle East
östlich (westlich) von . . . liegen, a, e — to lie to the east (west) of . . .
südlich (nördlich) von — south (north) of
die Breite; die Länge — latitude; longitude
zehn Grad nördlicher Breite — in latitude 10° N.
die südliche Halbkugel — Southern Hemisphere

364 [110–12]

weit entfernt — far away
unentwickelte Völker — undeveloped countries
unabhängig *or* **selbstständig** — independent, autonomous
im Ausland, in der Fremde[2] — abroad
fremd — strange, foreign, unknown
der (ein) Fremde(r) — stranger, foreigner
der Fremdenverkehrsverband, ¨e — tourist association (*for information in Germany*)
der Tourist, en, en — tourist
das Reisebüro, s — tourist agency
der britische Staatenbund — British Commonwealth

365 [118, 121]

rechnen — to calculate, do sums
um-rechnen — to convert
ab-rechnen — to deduct, subtract; *also* settle accounts
an-rechnen — to charge to someone's account
die Rechnung — calculation; *also* bill
berechnen — to compute, calculate
der elektronische Berechner — electronic computer
die Rechenmaschine — calculating machine
der Zirkel — compasses
der Gradbogen *or* **Winkelmesser** — protractor

[1] Cf. group 275.
[2] Cf. **Ins Ausland (in die Fremde) gehen,** to go abroad.

366 [124–7]

das Rätsel riddle, problem, puzzle [ful
problematisch *or* **zweifelhaft** problematic, doubt-
(sich) auf-lösen to dissolve (dissolve *intr.*)
der Rohstoff, e raw material
die Versuchanstalt experimental station
der Sauerstoff oxygen
der Stickstoff nitrogen
der Wasserstoff hydrogen
die Lebenslehre biology
der Techniker *or* **Facharbeiter** technician

THE ARTS

367 [136–9]

der Dirigent, en, en conductor
dirigieren to conduct, direct, lead
die Kammermusik chamber music
der Kapellmeister bandmaster
das Saxophon, e saxophone
die Klarinette clarinet
die Posaune trombone
die Operette *or* **leichte Oper** light opera, musical
das Opernhaus, ¨er opera house [comedy
in die Oper gehen, i, a to go to the opera

368 [139–40]

der Tanzsaal, -säle dance hall, ballroom
der Tänzer, (-in) dancer
das Tanzturnier, e dancing contest
der Walzer waltz
das Ballett, e ballet [ballet dancer
die Ballerina, -inen; Ballettänzerin ballerina;
die Variétévorstellung variety show
der Bauchredner ventriloquist
der Zauberer (-in) conjuror, magician (sorceress)
die Zauberei magic, witchcraft

369 [140]

der Zirkus, se circus
der Zirkusdirektor, en ringmaster
der Clown, s clown
das Drahtseil, das gespannte Seil tight-rope
der Seiltänzer tight-rope walker
das Trapez, e trapeze
der Akrobat, en, en acrobat
das Haus ist ausverkauft the house is sold out (*theatre*)
der Vorhang[1] geht auf (fällt) the curtain rises (falls)
der Zuschauerraum, ¨e auditorium

370 [140–2]

der Wandelgang, die -halle foyer
die Garderobe cloakroom
der erste (zweite) Rang, ¨e dress (upper) circle
der dritte Rang gallery
der Dramatiker playwright
der Regisseur, e producer; film director
der Akt *or* **Aufzug, ¨e** act
die Szene, der Auftritt, e scene
der Schlager; das Schlaglied, er hit; hit song
die Schlagerparade hit parade

371 [142]

das Gram(m)ophon, e gramophone
der Plattenspieler record-player
die Schallplatte gramophone record
die Langspielplatte long-playing record
der Schall, e *or* **¨e** sound (*generally*)
der Klang, ¨e sound (*musical*)
der Laut, e sound (*speech*)
der Ton, ¨e sound, note (*mus.*), tone
das Tonband, ¨er magnetic *or* sound-recording tape
das Tonbandgerät, e tape-recorder

[1] Note **der eiserne Vorhang,** the safety curtain (*theatre*) or iron curtain (*between East and West*).

372 [142, 145–6]

auf-nehmen, a, o, i to record
das Mikrophon, e microphone
die Spieltruhe juke-box [formance
ununterbrochene Vorstellung continuous per-
der Farbfilm, e technicolour film
die Großaufnahme close-up
der Filmgroße, Bühnenstern film *or* stage star
die Wochenschau newsreel
der Kulturfilm, e documentary film
der Reisefilm travelogue

373 [146]

die Platzanweiserin usherette
der Notausgang, ¨e emergency exit
das Radio radio, wireless
der Rundfunk broadcasting, radio
der Rundfunksender wireless transmitter
die Sendung[1] transmission, broadcast
die Schallplattenübertragung record programme
das Rundfunkgerät, e *or* **der Radioapparat, e**
das Hör- *or* **Sendespiel** radio play [wireless set
die Lang-, Mittel-, Kurzwellen, *f.pl.*
long, medium, short waves

374

die Wellenlänge wavelength
die (Zimmer)Antenne (indoor) aerial
der Lautsprecher loudspeaker [reception
einen guten Empfang bekommen to get good
die Störung, Störungen disturbance, atmospherics
der Abstimmungsknopf, ¨e tuning knob,
ab-stimmen auf (*acc.*) to tune in to [selector
an- (ab-)stellen to turn on (off), switch on (off)
ich höre gern Hörfolgen *f.pl.* I like features
Vorträge und Berichterstattungen talks and
commentaries

[1] Senden is regular when meaning 'to broadcast'.

375

auf Paris um-schalten to switch over to Paris
der Ansager *or* **Rundfunksprecher** announcer
Wir geben Nachrichten Here is the news
der Wetterbericht, e weather report
die Wettervoraussage weather forecast
die Radiogebühr wireless licence
das Radioreparaturgeschäft, e wireless repair
nicht in Ordnung out of order [shop
es (ihn, sie) in Ordnung bringen to put it right
die Röhren erneuern to renew the valves

376

das Fernsehen *or* **der Bildfunk** television
der Fernsehapparat, e television set
durch Fernsehen übertragen, u, a, ä to televise
der Fernsehbetrachter *or* **-teilnehmer** viewer
betrachten to look at, watch television
die Fernsehröre *or* **Bild-** television tube
der Fernsehschirm television screen
die Fernsehreklame television advertising
das Programm ein-stellen to switch on
der Fernsehsenderaum, ¨e television studio

377

die Photographie[1] photograph(y)
der Photograph, en, en photographer
die Filmkamera, s cine camera
die Kleinbildkamera; 35 mm. camera
der Schwarzweißfilm black and white film
scharf ein-stellen to focus, bring into focus
nicht scharf eingestellt out of focus, not sharp
die (Zeit)Aufnahme (time) exposure, photo-
die Momentaufnahme snapshot [graph
der (Probe)Abzug, ¨e (proof) print

[1] There is today a purist movement afoot to germanize spelling of Greek words such as **Fotografie, Telefon, Telegrafie,** etc.

378

die Bilder sind über-(unter-)belichtet the photos are over-(under-)exposed
die Belichtung exposure
das Negativ, e negative
entwickeln to develop
vergrössern to enlarge; *also* increase
sich photographieren lassen to have one's photo taken
das Objektiv, e lens
das Lichtbild *or* **Dia(positiv)** slide, transparency
der Projektionsapparat, e projector
die Leinwand, ¨e screen

379 [148–50]

Sport treiben,[1] **ie, ie** to go in for sports
einen Record brechen, a, o, i to break a record
der Wettkämpfer athlete, prize-fighter
das Wettspiel, e match, game, tournament
die Olympischen Spiele Olympic Games
mit . . . konkurrieren um to compete with . . . for
der Rudersport rowing
das Paddeln canoeing
das Wettrudern boat race
das Segelboot, e sailing boat

380 [150–1]

der Segelsport sailing, yachting
das Hallenbad, ¨er indoor swimming bath
das Schwimmbad *or* **-becken** swimming pool
die Badeanstalt baths
der Bergsteiger mountaineer
klettern‡ to climb
der Kletterer climber
der Rodelschlitten toboggan
rodeln to toboggan, sledge
der Bob(schlitten), Bobsleigh bobsleigh

[1] Cf. Sprachen treiben, to go in for languages.

381 [151]

die Bobmannschaft	bobsleigh crew
die (Hallen)Eisbahn	(covered) ice rink, skating rink
der Schi,[1] er	ski
der Skiläufer	skier
(Wasser)Schi laufen,† ie, au, äu	to (water)ski
der Steigbügel	stirrup
der Sporn, -ren	spur
die Reitgerte	riding whip
das Hindernisrennen	steeplechase
der Favorit, en, en	favourite

382 [151]

der Außenseiter	outsider
der Buchmacher	bookmaker
der Fußballspieler	footballer
der Fußballplatz, ¨e	football ground
der Schiedsrichter	referee, umpire
unentschieden enden	to end in a draw[2]
scheiden, ie, ie	to divide, separate
die Mannschaft	team
der Torwart, e	goalkeeper
die Halbzeit	half-time

383 [151–2]

der Strafstoß, ¨e	penalty kick
ein Tor erzielen[3]	to score a goal
Wie steht das Spiel?	What is the score?
die Schluß- *or* **Endrunde, das Endspiel**	cup final
die Vorschlußrunde	semi-final
der Tennisplatz, ¨e	tennis court
der Aufschlag, ¨e	service
auf-schlagen, u, a, ä	to serve
das Doppelspiel; Einzel-	doubles; singles
der Einstand, ¨e	deuce

[1] Also spelt **Ski,** *pl.* **Skier,** but always pronounced as English *she*.
[2] Cf. to draw a game, **ein Spiel unentschieden machen.**
[3] From **das Ziel, e,** target, aim, objective.

384 [152]

Null[1]	love, nil
das Federballspiel	badminton
das englische Schlagballspiel	cricket
der Schläger[2]**; das Schlagholz**	batsman; bat [(*cricket*)
der Werfer	bowler
der Stierkampf (-¨er)	bullfight (bullfighter)
die Stierarena, -nen	bullring
das Golf(spiel)	golf
der Golfplatz, ¨e	golf course, links
der Golfschläger[2]	golf club

385 [152]

der Abschlag, ¨e	tee
den Ball ab-schlagen	to tee off, drive
die Sandgrube	bunker
den Ball putten *or* **ein-lochen**	to putt
das Grün *or* **der (Golf)Spielrasen**	putting green
der Ringkämpfer *or* **Ringer**	wrestler
der Sekundant, en, en	second
der Conférencier[3]	announcer, the M.C.

Dies ist ein achtrundenkampf in je fünfminutenrunden. This is an 8-round contest of 5 minutes [each round.

386 [152]

Zwei Fälle, zwei Aufgaben oder ein Knock-out wird den Sieger entscheiden. Two falls, two submissions or a knockout will decide the winner.[4]

ausgeschlossen	disqualified
der Box- *or* **Faustkampf, ¨e**	boxing match
nieder- *or* **K.O.- schlagen, u, a, ä**	to knock out
ausgepunktet	beaten on points
nach Punkten siegen	to win on points
das Feder-, Leicht-, Mittelgewicht, e	feather, light, medium-weight
die Schwergewichtsmeisterschaft	heavyweight championship

[1] **beide Null!** love all.
[2] Cf. **Schläger** in group 152.
[3] Pron. as in French.
[4] The loser is **der Verlierer** *or* **Besiegete.**

387 [152]

seinen Titel verteidigen	to defend one's title
der Schieds- *or* **Ringrichter**	referee, umpire
er wurde ausgezählt	he was counted out
der Wettlauf, ¨e	foot race
der Hürdenlauf	hurdle race
der Staffellauf	relay race
die Leichtathletik	athletics
die Turnhalle	gymnasium
der Hochsprung, ¨e	high jump
der Weitsprung	long jump

388 [152–3]

der Stabhochsprung	pole vault
die Hantel	dumb-bell
der Gewichtheber	weightlifter
das Kugelstoßen	putting the shot
der Diskuswurf, ¨e	throwing the discus
das Speerwerfen	throwing the javelin
der Pfeilschütze, n, n	archer
Bogen mit Pfeilen	bow and arrows
der Kradfahrer	motor cyclist
das Beiwagenkrad[1]	motor cycle with sidecar

389 [153]

der Rennwagen	racing car
das Autofahren	motoring
der Motorroller	motor scooter
der Last(kraft)wagen	(motor) lorry
der Koffer	boot; *also* trunk
das Verdeck, e	hood; *also* deck
der Lenkrad, ¨er	steering wheel
die Wind(schutz)scheibe	windscreen
der Verbrennungsmotor, en	internal combustion engine
der Kühler	radiator (*car*)

[1] **Krad** for **Kraftrad,** *lit.* power-cycle.

390 [153]

der Reifen	tyre
das Ersatzrad, ¨er	sparewheel
die (Reifen)Panne	breakdown (puncture)
der Getriebekasten, ¨-	gearbox
der erste Gang, ¨e	bottom gear
schalten	to change gear
der Gashebel	accelerator
das Benzin, e	petrol
die Tankstelle	petrol pump, filling station
die Bremse; bremsen	brake; to brake

391 [154]

das Flugwesen	aviation
das Düsenflugzeug, e	jet plane
die Schallgeschwindigkeitsgrenze	speed of the sound barrier
der Doppeldecker	bi-plane
die Luftschraube; Schiffsschraube	propeller; screw *or* ship's propeller
flugtüchtig	airworthy
die Luftstewardeß, (ss)en	air hostess
der Pilot; Flieger	pilot; airman
der Flughafen, ¨-	aerodrome, airport
die Startbahn, Lande-	runway (*take off and landing*)

392 [154]

auf-steigen,† ie, ie *or* starten†	to take off
(glücklich) landen†	to land (make a safe landing)
notlanden†	to make a forced landing
der Flughafenkontrollturm, ¨e	airport traffic control tower
der Anschnallgurt, e	seat belt, safety belt
der (Steuer)Knüppel	joystick, control lever
stromlinienförmig	streamlined
gleiten,† i, i	to glide
der Gleitflug, ¨e	glide, gliding flight
der Jugendherberge	youth hostel

INTELLECTUAL AND MORAL LIFE

393 [161, 174–5]

begabt	gifted, talented
der Ehrenbürger	honorary citizen, freeman
das Ehren(denk)mal, ¨er	monument, cenotaph
das Ehrenwort, e	word of honour
Auf Ehre!	Upon my honour!
ihm zu Ehren	in his honour
ehrenhaft, -voll, -wert	honourable, creditable, respectable
ehrlos	dishonourable
ehrenamtlich	honorary (*i.e. unpaid*)
ehrenamtlicher Schriftführer	honorary secretary

SOCIETY

394 [185–6]

Heimweh haben	to be homesick
deutsch von Geburt	German by birth
ein gebürtiger *or* **geborener Berliner**	a native of Berlin
die Autobahn	motorway
der Verkehrszeichen	traffic sign
die Verkehrsampeln, *f.pl.*	traffic lights
die Verkehrsstockung	traffic jam *or* block
der Durchgangsverkehr	through traffic
der Straßenknotenpunkt, e	road junction
der Kreuzweg, e	crossroads

395 [186–7, 189]

Parken verboten!	No parking!
der Parkplatz, ¨e	parking place
die Einbahnstraße	one way street
die Doppelkurve	double *or* Z-bend
die Umleitung	diversion
(ab-)sperren	to close, barricade, block
auf-sperren	to unlock, open wide
die Straßensperre	road block
Vorsicht! *or* **Achtung!**	Caution!, Attention!
das Kaffeehaus, ¨er	café, coffee house

396 [190–1, 196]

die Befriedung(spolitik)	appeasement
die Diktatur	dictatorship
der Diktator, en; -isch	dictator; dictatorial
der Staatsstreich, e	coup d'état
das allgemeine Stimmrecht	universal suffrage
der Wähler	voter, elector
zur Wahl gehen,† i, a	to go to the poll
stimmen für	to vote for
645 Stimmen	645 votes
die Abstimmung *or* **das Stimmenresultat**	voting poll

397 [212–13]

der Feiertag, e	holiday, day of rest
der Geburtstag; Namens-	birthday; s.o.'s name day
der Karneval *or* **Fasching**[1]	carnival (*before Lent*)
das Fasten *or* **die Fastenzeit**	Lent
Pfingstsonntag	Whitsunday, Pentecost
die Maifeier	May Day, (*1st May*)
der Muttertag	Mother's Day (*1st Sunday in May*)
Allerheiligen	All Saints' Day, All Hallows' (*1st Nov.*)
Allerseelen	All Souls' Day (*Cath. 2nd Nov.*)
Totensonntag	Remembrance Sunday

398 [221–2, 227–30]

der Matrose, n	rating, sailor
der Kran, ⁻̈e	crane, derrick
der Bohrturm, ⁻̈e	derrick (*oil-well*)
die Flucht ergreifen, i, i	to take to flight
die Spionage	espionage, spying
jemanden nach-spionieren	to spy on somebody
der Kriegsgefangene	prisoner of war
das Internierungslager	internment camp
die Folter	rack, torture
foltern	to torture, torment

1 Karneval in Rhineland; Fasching in Bavaria and Austria.

399 [232]

die Luftwaffe[1]	airforce
der Luftangriff, e	air raid
die Luftlandetruppen	airborne troops
die Flugbrücke	airlift
der Fallschirm, e	parachute
die Fallschirmtruppen	paratroops
die Rakete	rocket
das ferngesteuerte Geschoß, e	guided missile
das Atom; die -bombe	atom; atomic bomb
die Ortung	position finding (*radar*)

SOCIAL ACTIVITY

400 [233–9, 241–3, 248]

der Landarbeiter	farm labourer
der Trecker[2]	(farm) tractor
der Mähdrescher	combine harvester
der Hopfen	hop
der Flachs	flax
(un)bezahlter Urlaub	holiday with(out) pay
auf Abzahlung kaufen	to buy on hire purchase
das Blindschreiben	touch-typing
das Diktiergerät, e	dictaphone
vervielfältigen	to duplicate

401 [248, 255, 266, 268]

der Vervielfältigungsapparat, e	duplicator
das Kohlepapier, e	carbon paper
der Barscheck, s	open, uncrossed cheque
der gekreuzte Scheck	crossed cheque [strike
in den Streik treten, a, e, i	to come out *or* go on
den Streik ab-brechen, a, o, i	to call off the strike
das Selbstbedienungsgeschäft	self service store
die freie Wirtschaft	private enterprise
der Automat, en, en	slot machine
selbsttätig *or* automatisch	automatic

[1] Cf. R.A.F., die englische Luftwaffe; the German airforce, die deutsche Luftwaffe. [2] i.e. motor-traction engine; Schlepper is anything that hauls, see group 223.

402 [268–9]

die chemische Reinigung dry cleaning
die Reinigungsanstalt dry cleaner's
das Reinigungsmittel detergent
die automatische Waschanstalt launderette
die Rolltreppen *f.pl.* escalator
der Fahrstuhl, ¨e lift
Bitte Haare schneiden! Haircut, please!
Ich möchte mein Haar gewaschen und onduliert haben. I want my hair shampooed and set.
das Haarwaschmittel shampoo
die Wasserwelle set

403 [269, 271–3]

die Dauerwelle perm(anent wave)
die Locke curl
der Föhn, e hair dryer[1]
die Nagelpflege; Fuß- manicure; chiropody
das Hühnerauge, n corn (*on foot*)
die Nagellack, e nail varnish
die Gesichtsbehandlung facial treatment
der Bahnwärter signalman
der Durchgangswagen through carriage
der Gang, ¨e corridor, passage

404 [273–4, 277–9, 282]

besetzt *or* belegt occupied, engaged
reserviert reserved
die Gepäckaufbewarung left-luggage office
die Annahme; die Ausgabe deposit; withdrawal
ein Formular aus-füllen to fill in a form
der Empfangschein, e receipt (*in acknowledgment*)
amtlich *or* offiziell official
die Fernsprechstelle public telephone box
die Nummer- *or* Wählscheibe dial
die Nummer wählen to dial

[1] From the original meaning of **Föhn**, a warm south wind.

405 [282]

der (Telephon)Hörer	receiver
auf Summton warten	to wait for dialling tone
der Zahlknopf, ¨e	Button A (*pay-button*)
die Münzzurückgabe	Button B (*money return*)
der Telephonanruf *or* **das -gespräch, ¨e**	telephone call
der Fernanruf, e	trunk call
das Fernsprechamt, ¨er *or* **die Zentrale**	telephone exchange
das Telephonfraülein *or* **die Telephonistin**	telephone operator
Sie sind falsch verbunden	You have the wrong No.
das Telephon ist besetzt	the telephone is engaged

THE UNIVERSE

406 [283]

der Kosmos	universe, cosmos
der Astronaut, en, en *or* **Kosmosfahrer**	astronaut
der Weltraum, ¨e	space, universe
die Weltraumreise	space travel *or* journey
Flug um den Erdball	flight round the earth
die Weltreise	trip round the world (*on earth*)
um-kreisen	to circle, go round
das (Welt)Raumschiff, e	space vessel
die (Raum)Kapsel	(space) capsule
die Schwerkraft, ¨e	(force of) gravity

407 [283]

die Lufthülle *or* **Atmosphäre**	atmosphere
der Luftdruck, e	atmospheric pressure
atmosphärisch	atmospheric
der Trabant, en, en *or* **Satellit, en, en**	satellite
die Planetenbahn	orbit
der Komet, en, en	comet
der Sterndeuter *or* **Astrolog, en, en**	astrologer
die Sterndeuterei	astrology
der Sternforscher *or* **Astronom, en, en**	astronomer
die Sternkunde *or* **Gestirnlehre**	astronomy

408 [283–8, 293]

das Sternbild, er	constellation
die Sternschnuppe	shooting star
besternt *or* **gestirnt**	starry, starlit
mondhell	moonlit
der Vollmond; Halb-	full moon; crescent moon
das Fernrohr, e	telescope
der Vulkan, e	volcano
aus-brechen,† a, o, i	to erupt, break out
die Landenge	isthmus
die Nässe	dampness, humidity

ANIMALS

409 [296–7]

der Jagdhund, e	hunting dog
der Schäferhund[1]	sheepdog
die Bulldogge	bulldog
der Pudel	French poodle
der Dachshund *or* **Dackel**	dachshund, badgerdog
der Wachtelhund	spaniel
der Windhund	greyhound
der Stöberhund	retriever
die Koppel(leine)	leash
der Maulkorb, ¨e	muzzle

410 [299–302]

der Bock, ¨e	buck, he-goat
das Raubtier, e	beast of prey
der Pelz, e	fur
das Renntier	reindeer
das Eichhörnchen	squirrel
die Fledermaus, ¨e	bat
der Maulwurf, ¨e	mole
das Wiesel	weasel
der Rüssel	(*elephant's*) trunk
das Nilpferd, e	hippopotamus

[1]Cf. **deutscher Schäferhund,** Alsatian; **schottischer Schäferhund,** collie.

411 [302–5]

das Nashorn, ··er	rhinoceros
der Büffel	buffalo
die Giraffe	giraffe
die Gemse	chamois
der Stachel, n	sting, prickle; *also* thorn
der Ameisenhaufen	anthill
die Grille	cricket
der Floh, ··e	flea
die Laus, ··e	louse
die Wanze	bug

412 [305–7]

der Nachtfalter *or* **Nachtschmetterling**	moth
die (Kleider)Motte	(clothes') moth
von Motten zerfressen	moth-eaten
die Puppe	chrysalis; *also* doll, puppet
die Eidechse	lizard
das Krokodil, e	crocodile
die Riesenschlange	boa-constrictor
die Klapperschlange	rattlesnake
die Meise	tom-tit
der Wellensittich	budgerigar

413 [307–10]

Eier legen	to lay eggs
(aus-)brüten	to brood (hatch)
die Brut	brood, hatch, covey
die Drossel	thrush
die Krähe	crow, rook
der Habicht, e	hawk
der Specht, e *or* **Holzhacker**	woodpecker
der Fasan, e *or* **en**	pheasant
das Feldhuhn, ··er	partridge
das Waldhuhn *or* **Moor-**	grouse

414 [310–11]

die Möwe	seagull
der Eisvogel, ¨-	kingfisher
der (Fish)Reiher	heron
der Pinguin, e	penguin
entgräten[1]	to bone, fillet
der Schellfisch, e	haddock
der Kabeljau, e *or* s	cod
der Steinbutt, e	turbot
der Heilbutt, en	halibut
der Tintenfisch	cuttle-fish

415 [311–12]

der Hecht, e	pike
der Bück(l)ing, e	kipper
der Seepolyp, en, en	octopus
die Schnecke	snail
das Schneckenhaus, ¨er	snail's shell
die (Mies)Muschel	shell, conch (*mussel*)
die Herzmuschel	cockle
die (Stein)Garnele	shrimp (prawn)
der Seelöwe, n	sea lion
der Delphin, e	dolphin

PLANTS

416 [317–20]

die Narzisse	daffodil
das Schneeglöckchen	snowdrop
die (spanische) Wicke, n, *f.pl.*	sweet peas
das Gemüse	vegetables
der Gemüsehändler	greengrocer
der Spinat, e	spinach
die Linse	lentil
der Salat, e	salad
die (Brunnen)Kresse	(water)cress
der Knoblauch, e	garlic

[1] See Gräte in group 311.

417 [323–8]

die Melone melon
die Lesezeit vintage time
der Weinbau, e *or* ten vine-growing, vini-
der Weinbauer vine-grower [culture
der Weinhändler wine merchant
der Rohrzucker cane sugar
das Bambusrohr, e bamboo cane
der (das) Gummi *or* der Kautschuk rubber
der Weissdorn *or* Hagedorn hawthorn
der Tannenzapfen fir cone

MINERALS

418 [329, 334, 336]

der Bergbau mining industry, mining
das Schmiedeisen wrought iron
der Schiefer slate, schist
die Tonerde potter's clay
die Tonwaren *f.pl.* pottery, earthenware
die Tonarbeit *or* -kunst pottery, ceramics
der Töpfer potter
der Werkstoff, e substitute material, syn-
das plastische Material plastics [thetic plastics
das Kügelchen (aus Bernstein) (amber) bead

APPENDIX

DAYS OF THE WEEK

der Sonntag Sunday
der Montag Monday
der Dienstag Tuesday
der Mittwoch Wednesday
der Donnerstag Thursday
der Freitag Friday
der Samstag / **der Sonnabend** } Saturday

MONTHS

Januar January
Februar February
März March
April April
Mai May
Juni June
Juli July
August August
September September
Oktober October
November November
Dezember December

SEASONS

der Frühling, (e)s, e / **das Frühjahr, (e)s, e** } spring
der Sommer, s, – summer
der Herbst, es, e autumn
der Winter, s, – winter

NUMERALS

1 **eins (ein, eine, ein)**
2 **zwei**
3 **drei**
4 **vier**
5 **fünf**
6 **sechs**
7 **sieben**
8 **acht**
9 **neun**
10 **zehn**
11 **elf**
12 **zwölf**
13 **dreizehn**
14 **vierzehn**
15 **fünfzehn**
16 **sechzehn**
17 **siebzehn**
18 **achtzehn**
19 **neunzehn**
20 **zwanzig**

21 einundzwanzig
22 zweiundzwanzig
23 dreiundzwanzig
31 einunddreißig
40 vierzig
50 fünfzig
60 sechzig
70 siebzig
80 achtzig
90 neunzig
100 hundert
101 hundert(und)eins
102 hundert(und)zwei
110 hundert(und)zehn
200 zweihundert
300 dreihundert
1000 tausend
1001 tausend(und)eins
5000 fünftausend
10,000 zehntausend
100,000 hunderttausend
1,000,000 eine Million
5,000,000 fünf Millionen
1,000,000,000 eine Milliarde

1st der (die, das) erste
2nd der zweite
3rd der dritte
4th der vierte
5th der fünfte
8th der achte
10th der zehnte
11th der elfte
12th der zwölfte
20th der zwanzigste
21st der einundzwanzigste
22nd der zweiundzwanzigste
30th der dreißigste
100th der hundertste
101st der hundert(und)erste
200th der zweihundertste
1000th der tausendste
1,000,000th der millionste
last der (die, das) letzte

PREPOSITIONS

Governing the Genitive

(an)statt instead of
trotz in spite of
um . . . willen for the sake of
während during
-wegen on account of, because of

Governing the Dative

aus out of, from, of
außer except, besides
bei by, near, at, with
-gegenüber opposite
mit with, along with
nach after, to (*a place*), according to
seit since
von from, of, by (*agent*)
zu to (*a person*), at, for

Governing the Accusative

-ausgenommen except
bis till, to, as far as
durch through, by (means of
für for
gegen towards, against
ohne without, but for
um (a)round, about, for
wider against

Governing Dative or Accusative

(The Dative answers the question *where? in what place?* and therefore denotes position and rest, or motion within a place; while the accusative expresses motion to a place and answers the question *whither? where to?*—But whenever in doubt use accusative.)

an at, near, on, to
auf on, upon, to, for
hinter behind
in in, into
neben beside, near, with
über over, above, about
unter under, among
vor before, for, ago
zwischen between

MISCELLANEOUS

bitte please
gefälligst please
(bitte um) Verzeihung I beg your pardon
danke (sehr *or* schön) thanks
bitte (sehr *or* schön) don't mention it
das hängt davon ab it depends
das stimmt that is correct
es stimmt it is all right
recht (all)right
aufrecht up, standing
oben at the top, upstairs
unten at the bottom, downstairs
herein! come in
hinaus! go out
hinein! go in
heraus! come out
hierher (*come*) here
hinauf (*go*) upstairs
herunter (*come*) downstairs
daher from there, thence
hier here, this way
dort that way
fort! away!
sofort, sogleich immediately, at once
jetzt now
aufwärts upwards
abwärts downwards
vorwärts forwards, onwards
rückwärts backwards
auswärts outwards
vorn at *or* on the front
hinten at *or* on the back
mitten (in *d.*) in the middle
rechts at *or* to the right
links at *or* to the left
geradeaus straight on *or* ahead
diesseits *gen.* on this side
jenseits *gen.* beyond
drüben over yonder, over there
verkehrt turned the wrong way
außerhalb *gen.* outside of
innerhalb *gen.* inside of
oberhalb *gen.* above
unterhalb *gen.* below
darunter underneath
nebenan next door, close by
schnell quick, fast
langsam slowly
lange long, a long time
lange her long ago
kürzlich lately
neulich recently, the other day

damals at that time, then
spät late
früh early
früher formerly, sooner
bald soon
schon, bereits already
immer always
nie, niemals never
nimmermehr nevermore
niemand no one, nobody
nichts nothing
etwas something
etwa nearly, about
ungefähr about
mehrere several
oft often
selten seldom
häufig frequently
dann then
dann und wann now and then
wann? when?
wenn if, whenever, when
wenn auch even if
noch nicht not yet
nicht mehr no more, no longer
entweder . . . oder either—or
weder . . . noch neither—nor
vorher beforehand
nachher afterwards
im voraus in advance
vorbei past (*time*)
vorbei (an *d.*) past (*place*)
warum? why?
darum for this reason
weil because
deswegen / **deshalb** } therefore, for this *or* that reason
meinetwegen for my sake
wieviel (-viele) how much (— many)
ein wenig a little
vielleicht perhaps
vielmehr rather, on the contrary
lieber rather, more gladly
gern gladly, willingly
ungern unwillingly
sonst else, otherwise
sonst etwas anything else
sonst nichts nothing else
umsonst for nothing, in vain
vergebens in vain
bloß barely, simply, only
nur only, but
nicht nur . . . sondern auch not only . . . but also
zusammen together
beisammen together
auseinander asunder, apart
aufeinander on another, against one another
anders otherwise
etwas anders something else
genug enough
-gemäß *dat.* according to
betreffend *acc.* about, concerning
weit, fern far
bei weitem by far
bei weitem nicht not nearly
beinahe, fast nearly, almost
nahe *dat.* near
überall everywhere
irgendwo somewhere
anderswo elsewhere
besonders especially
meistens mostly
gewöhnlich usually, generally
gänzlich wholly, entirely
ganz quite
teilweise partly
leider unfortunately, sad to say
glücklicherweise fortunately
durchaus throughout, absolutely, by all means
durchaus nicht / **keineswegs** } by no means, in no way
unterwegs (nach) on the way (to)

natürlich of course
gewiß surely, certainly
wirklich really
überhaupt at all
gar nicht not at all
nicht einmal not even
im Gegenteil on the contrary
im allgemeinen in general
allein alone; only
einzeln one by one, separately
einfach one-fold; simple
zweifach two-fold
zuerst (at) first
zuletzt last
endlich at last
erstens in the first place
zweitens in the second place
einst once, some day
einmal once (upon a time)
auf einmal all at once
zweimal twice
jedesmal every time
manchmal several times, sometimes, often
zum ersten Mal for the first time
zum letzten Mal for the last time
aufs nächste Mal for the next time
einerlei of the same kind
zweierlei of two different kinds
mancherlei of many kinds
allerlei all kinds of
was für ein (eine) what kind of
anfangs at the beginning
zuweilen sometimes, occasionally
heutzutage nowadays
künftig in the future
vorläufig for the present
geläufig fluently
zufällig by chance *or* accident
jedenfalls at all events, in any case
falls in case
ebenfalls } likewise
gleichfalls } likewise
nachts at night
bei Tag by day
mittags at noon
Sonntags on Sundays
am Sonntag on Sunday
vor acht Tagen a week ago
vor vierzehn Tagen a fortnight ago
vier Tage lang for four days
seit drei Tagen these (last) three days
den ganzen Tag all day long
zweimal des Tages twice a day
eine Zeitlang for a time
auf einige Zeit for a while (*future*)
auf Wiedersehen good-bye
auf Wiederhören (*radio*) good-bye